A FULL QUIVER

CHOOSE LIFE
P.O. Box 1435
Orange Park, FL 32067-1435
(904) 777-2266

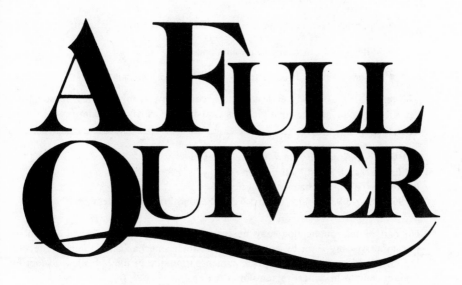

A FULL QUIVER

RICK & JAN HESS

Foreword By Mary Pride

*Family Planning And
The Lordship of Christ*

Wolgemuth & Hyatt, Publishers, Inc.
Brentwood, Tennessee

The mission of Wolgemuth & Hyatt, Publishers, Inc. is to publish and distribute books that lead individuals toward:

- A personal faith in the one true God: Father, Son, and Holy Spirit;

- A lifestyle of practical discipleship; and

- A worldview that is consistent with the historic, Christian faith.

Moreover, the Company endeavors to accomplish this mission at a reasonable profit and in a manner which glorifies God and serves His Kingdom.

© 1989 by Rick and Jan Hess. All rights reserved
Published March 1990. First Edition
Printed in the United States of America
97 96 95 94 93 92 91 90   8 7 6 5 4 3 2 (Second Printing, September 1990)

Unless otherwise noted, all Scripture quotations are from the New American Standard Bible, copyrighted by The Lockman Foundation 1960, 1962, 1963, 1968, 1971, 1972, 1973, 1975, 1977 and are used by permission.

Wolgemuth & Hyatt, Publishers, Inc.
1749 Mallory Lane, Suite 110, Brentwood, Tennessee 37027.

Library of Congress Cataloging-in-Publication Data

Hess, Rick
      A full quiver : family planning and the lordship of Christ / Rick
and Jan Hess.
         p. cm.
      ISBN 0-943497-83-3
      1. Birth control — Religious aspects — Christianity. 2. Family
size — Religious aspects. I. Hess, Jan. II. Title.
HQ766.25.H47   1990
304.6'66 — dc20   90-30994
                                                                        CIP

Dedicated with all our love
to our parents,
Robert and Helen Hess
and Russell and Lou Nash,
the best grandquivers
our arrows could have

Contents

ACKNOWLEDGMENTS

T his book should be entitled Volume II, Volume I being a list of those people to whom we are indebted for their help and encouragement. The following people were of special help in this work: Randy and Peggy Johnson, who started us thinking and proved sanity was quite possible with six children; Dianne Cosgrove, mother of six, who did an excellent job of proofreading and editing our original manuscript five years ago without laughing out loud (how was I to know that *is* and *am* were not interchangeable?).

The following people read the manuscript at various times and gave us very candid observations, criticisms, suggestions and encouragement: Carl and Leona Anderson, David and Laurie Baratta, Merlin and Peggy Davis, Ron and Sherry Dick, Gary Fraley, Charlie and Lauri Fritz, Steve and Deb Hughes, Don and Peg Johnston, Steve and Terri Johnston, Alan and Dorothy Kucera, Loran and Candy Presley, Jim and Dian Shaul, Jim and Laura Stearn, Ward and Sharon Sutton; Doug and Gerry Holiday of Holigraphics (two years ago they told me to take one of their computers home for the weekend and put this book into it. I'd still be punching keys on my typewriter without them — and their disks, laser printers, knowledge and time); our editor at Wolgemuth & Hyatt, Darryl Winburne, who did an outstanding job on this project.

Most of all, thanks to Mary Pride, our book agent and one whose pen graces more than a few pages in this book. Though we have only met her, her husband Bill, and their seven children long distance, we love and feel a strong kinship with them — allies in the War. Thank you Mary.

FOREWORD

I am pleased, proud, happy, and delighted to introduce this wonderful book by Rick and Jan Hess! Ever since the day I got a phone call from a total stranger named Rick Hess who wanted to tell me about the new book he and Jan had written, I have been eagerly anticipating the day *A Full Quiver* would come out.

I promise you, this is *not* just another Christian book! "Life-changing" and "exciting" about sum it up — as do "Biblical," "refreshing," and even "entertaining." Nothing slays the dragons of doubt and depression like a good dose of laughter. And what could be more contagious than the Hess's faith and joy — especially when applied to an issue that we usually think of with worry and fear for the future?

Rick and Jan remind us that we can trust God to plan our lives for us better than we can ourselves. Nothing novel here — but the *application* of this truth to family planning and their Biblical teaching on the blessing of children produce some surprises!

I don't endorse this book lightly. For one thing, I have been living it for the past thirteen years, before Rick and Jan even wrote it! From our experience and the experience of thousands of families that have written to us, my husband Bill and I can confidently assert that the fruit of this teaching is *good*. Those who don't try it may knock it, but those who are willing to work at being good stewards of those blessings know better!

A Full Quiver may not bring revival all by itself (although who am I to limit God by saying it won't?), but it sure as shootin' will dispel a lot of the clammy fog that is crippling the church's evangelistic and discipling efforts in our generation.

What an effect this book could have on our churches, communities, social institutions, and families!

Every Christian couple — and I mean *you* — will be blessed when we all finally rediscover the long-dormant principles outlined in this book.

Yours truly,
Mary Pride

INTRODUCTION

W e've decided not to have any more children." "We wish we had waited longer before we had our second." "We're waiting until my husband is finished with school." How often have you heard comments like these? We need no hidden microphones to collect these nuggets. They can be found almost everywhere: at the laundromat, at the next Tupperware party, at baby showers, at the spa, in the pew behind you in church. You can hear this philosophy from work associates, friends, or relatives. You may have even made such remarks yourself — we did!

When we were newlyweds, I (Rick) was in graduate school, and we decided that we should not have children during that time. We never really talked in depth about our decision. We just did what everyone else was doing, without thinking too much about it.

After graduation our first child, Staci, was born, and in our hearts a tiny spark of questioning was ignited which later turned into a full-fledged blaze of confusion and uncertainty. Should we have any more children? How many? What spacing? Why was so little help available to assist us in making such an important decision? Was the decision even *our* responsibility?

During the years following Staci's arrival, we wrestled and wondered in our souls. We also sought counsel from anyone who would give it. If we talked to twenty people, it seemed we received twenty different answers. Finally, after our fourth child, Stefani, was born, people began *freely* giving us counsel!

In the past five years we have studied and meditated on God's Word and feel now that at least to a small degree we comprehend His plan for marriage and the church more clearly than we did when we were first married. We would like to present to you the path over which God has led us and the conclusions we live by today.

But first, let us introduce ourselves to you.

I enjoy sports such as racquetball and tennis. I also collect games and love to be with Jan (these things are not listed in order of preference!). A list of Jan's favorite things would include going for walks, reading, date night, and talking about our children. To the best of our knowledge, neither of us is revered as one of the great minds of Western civilization. My resumé has no citations for Rhodes scholarships, Mensa memberships, Nobels, Pulitzers, Oscars, Heisman Trophies, or *Who's Who* inclusions (a listing is pending in *What's That?*). So you see, we are just your average Midwestern couple . . . with eight children.

"Eight children!" Yes, praise God — eight (count 'em!) children in our quiver. You see, God showed us something new about children — something we had never heard before. He showed us that children *are* a blessing once we learned *why* children are a blessing and *how* to benefit from that blessing. He showed us how we could greatly increase our spiritual usefulness and power, prepare for revival in our culture, and get closer to Him by properly employing the blessing of children. He also showed us that it's not whether your family ends

up large or small that makes the difference, but whether you *know what the blessing is* and how to find it.

God has given us such joy as we look at our little blessings romping around the yard or "ranged" around the table. We long to share this joy and the other special blessings we'll be talking about in this book with you. May God enable you to read this book with the special vision that comes from desiring that all of our ways be in His capable hands — and may He *bless* you!

Helpful Tools

We have included some tools to help you understand, focus on, and consider the subject of this book. We hope that you will find them useful for yourself and for group study.

First, there are three appendixes.

Appendix A is an explanation of the problems of Biblical thinking in a rationalistic culture. Read it for a more in-depth view of the aspects of probability and statistics.

Appendix B can be used right away. We encourage you to become amateur surveyors! Before beginning this book, complete the survey in Appendix B. There are sixteen questions to answer if you are single and twenty-two if married. The engaged single reader is encouraged to have his/her "sweetie" take this. Compare your answers.

Appendix C is a Discussion Leader's Guide with ideas on how to use this book in a class setting. A discussion leader will find it full of sample questions, additional Biblical references, and creative fodder.

Second, each chapter ends with a section called "Focus." These sections will challenge, inspire, and motivate you to further thinking and reading.

Focus

Let's begin to focus your thinking with three questions to prepare you for chapter one:

- What is your family size philosophy? (Include your reasons and Scriptural support.)

- Where do attitudes about family size originate?

- How much input from parents and friends have you had in the area of birth control?

1

"WE JUST LOVE OUR KIDS"
OR DO WE?

The story is told of a man who had a reputation for really loving children. Let's call him Jake. Jake always had candy in his pocket for any children he might happen to meet, and a kindly pat on the head for any child he passed. He never said an unkind word about a child. Rather, he seemed to delight in the sight of them playing happily on the sidewalk in front of his house.

One day Jake needed to have a new sidewalk poured. After the workmen had left, he got down on his hands and knees and carefully smoothed the surface, putting the little decorative ridges just where he wanted them. Then he sat down on his porch for a well-deserved rest and drink of lemonade.

But, unhappily for Jake, school had just let out. Swarms of children suddenly appeared, tromping on his not-yet-hardened sidewalk and riding over it with their bikes. In less time than it takes to tell, his beautiful sidewalk looked like something even a modern artist couldn't love.

Red with fury, Jake leaped off his chair. "You no-good, lousy, rotten kids! Can't you see I just poured that sidewalk and it isn't dry? Get away from it!" He could be heard all over the neighborhood.

Jake's next door neighbor opened his screen door and stepped out. "Hey, Jake," he called, "how come you're ranting and raving like this? I thought you loved kids."

"I love 'em all right," Jake shot back. "I love 'em in the abstract, but *not* in the concrete!" (Or at least not in *his* concrete!)

Christians today are sure we love kids. We give generously whenever someone flashes a picture of a sad-eyed orphan before us. We crusade against child abuse. We goo and gurgle at the new babies in church. But are we like Jake, who loved kids in the abstract but not in the concrete? Do we *really* like to have them around? Or are we like the rabbi in the great musical *Fiddler on the Roof,* who prayed "God bless and keep the Csar—far away from us!"? Do we hope God will bless and keep the kids far, far away—in the nursery, in the day care center, in school, or at summer camp? Or maybe even that He will keep us from having any in the first place (and certainly not more than one or two!)?

➻   ➻   ➻

Here are some snapshots to help you determine just how valued children really are in our world today.

Snapshot One

Two people are making noise in the church service. One is old Mr. Lewis, who suffers from smoker's cough developed over forty years. He sits hacking and wheezing, loudly snorting into his handkerchief, and moving about in his seat from time to time to get more comfortable. The other is little Baby Bethy on her mother's lap. Bethy lets out an occasional "goo" that can be heard all over the sanctuary.

Questions

- Who gets the disapproving glares, old Mr. Lewis or Bethy's mother?

- Who do others in the church strongly suggest should be kept somewhere else during the service?

- *Who* is making the most noise?

Snapshot Two

You are at the mall, enjoying an afternoon's shopping. Seated in the center area is a young mother with five lively children, some of whom are obviously beginning to feel the strain of a long shopping expedition. Your feet are killing you, and the only place you can sit is next to them. So you sit down, clutching your shopping bags. She smiles at you, and you feel you must say something.

Question

Which do you say:

- (Pointing at the children and counting loudly) "One! Two! Three! Four! FIVE! They sure must keep you busy!"

- "You must have your hands full!"

- "What a BIG family! Are they ALL yours?"

- "What lovely children! You must be very proud to have such a nice, large family!"

Snapshot Three

The Mall, Part Two: The young mother, whose name you find out is Jennifer, has just told you that yes, they are all hers.

Question

Which is your reply (pick one)?

- "I'm sure glad it's you and not me!"

- "How *can* you afford them all?"

- "How many *more* children do you plan to have?"

- "That might be fine for you, but two is more than enough for me!"

- "Five! Haven't you figured out what causes that?" or "Haven't you heard of birth control?" or "Haven't you heard of overpopulation?"

- "Don't you believe in family planning?"

- "Five of your own! What a blessing!"

Snapshot Four

Jennifer is no longer at the mall. She, her husband, and her five children are at church. Jennifer has just found out that she is expecting her sixth and informs her friends in the women's Sunday School class of this. After church, one of them comes up and says something to Jennifer.

Question

Which do you think she does?

- Rejoices with Jennifer over her sixth pregnancy?

- Teases Jennifer about breeding *like a rabbit* and/or being ignorant of basic family planning techniques?

- Chides Jennifer for not having more sense and urges her to have herself or her husband *fixed* this time?

How often have you heard a woman complaining that her children drive her crazy/she couldn't stand staying home all day with them/she isn't planning on having any more because she is having trouble handling those she has? How often have you heard a mother making these complaints *in front of* her children?

➤ ➤ ➤

We believe that as you read this book, you will become more aware of the high value God places on children. You will also become more sensitive to the great gulf between the Bible's teaching about children and our own culture's attitude. You will learn how the church can recover a truly welcoming attitude towards children — and the huge difference this can make in our effectiveness in this world. (Not to mention how much more encouraging it would be for poor Jennifer!) You will learn about God's special plan to make each of *your own* children a blessing.

Focus

In this chapter we looked at different attitudes people have toward children. How would you answer the following questions?

- Do most families plan their evenings around spending personal time with their children?

- Do most Christian parents expect their children to grow up as solid Christians, and will they make any sacrifice it takes to see this happen?

- Do pastors routinely give instructions in their Mother's Day sermons on how to encourage parents with large families?

- Do Christians have extremely different attitudes about children than non-Christians?

The first and one of the most important questions dealt with in this book is: Where do babies come from? What comes to your mind as a reply? Let us start right now with a look at the Bible's surprising answer.

2

WHERE DO BABIES COME FROM?
(It's an Open and Shut Case)

W here do babies come from, Mama?" Children are smart about asking all the important questions, aren't they? What we believe about the origin of life — particularly where children come from — can either help us to find or lead us to miss, many blessings, especially the blessing of a full quiver.

So where *do* babies come from? There are two ways to answer that question. A proponent of what we will call "Philosophy A" would say that babies are simply a product of a random meeting of sperm and egg. The tots so produced are wonderfully cute, certainly, but really they are only a function of biological probability, with personalities and talents determined solely by random chance. Those who hold to this also teach that parents are the only thinking, responsible agent behind the conception process. If this is true, it follows that we are the only ones who can and therefore should or must exercise control in conception. This is the philosophy that has led to seeing nothing horribly wrong with ending the existence of a random "product of conception," as the unborn child has been conveniently labeled. It also sees nothing wrong with performing experiments on these babies before and after birth, or "logically" for that matter when they grow up to be ninety years old and confined to a hospital bed. No blessings here!

Now it's time to meet "Philosophy B." This is where we come in. This concept is different. Really different. So different, in fact, that those in the Philosophy A camp cannot fathom why Philosophy B people believe what they do—except for one thing—they know it has something to do with the Bible and God.

But what is it in the Bible that runs contrary to the random probability theory held by so much of our society? Maybe you yourself believe that your own existence began solely at a chance uniting of a couple of cells. Please read on and discover the amazing truth!

We will not attempt to consider every Biblical passage that talks about conception here, but we will look at some important ones. So here we go, searching for help to answer the question: where do babies come from?

Old Testament Examples

Eve: "With the Help of the Lord."

We begin our study of beginnings near the beginning of the book of beginnings—Genesis, chapter four. Verse one provides the perfect starting point, as it records the first birth of a human being. Let's see how new mom Eve answers the question, "Where do babies come from?" When Cain is born she testifies, "I have gotten a manchild with the help of the LORD."

Eve, who had enjoyed a first-person relationship with God, speaks not as a lettered theologian but as a practicing mother. She fully realizes that God has been necessary for the birth of her son and that Cain's arrival did not happen without His intervention. This is an excellent starting point in our quest, as it is quite obvious that Eve believed God was involved in bringing about Cain's existence.

Hagar: God Does the Multiplying.

In Genesis 16 we find the angel of the Lord counseling Hagar, Abraham's exiled servant-wife. In verse 10 it reads: "Moreover, the angel of the LORD said to her, 'I will greatly multiply your descendants so that they shall be too many to count.' "

The angel of the Lord, speaking for God, said a very interesting thing. What he did *not* say is even more interesting. He did not tell Hagar, "You will have so many descendants that they shall be too many to count." He specifically said, "*I* will greatly multiply your descendants." God Himself was going to personally multiply these people.

Abraham: The Blessing.

The Abrahamic covenant is one of the landmark beacons in Scripture. In Genesis 17:2 God promises Abraham, "And I will establish My covenant between Me and you, and I will multiply you exceedingly."

The wording is again significant. God did *not* say, "You will multiply exceedingly" but assumed total responsibility for creating Abraham's descendants — "I will multiply you exceedingly."

Abimelech: God Closes the Wombs.

Our next stop is also in Genesis: chapter 20. We know well
the story of an embarrassed Abraham having to tell king
Abimelech that his step-sister was also his wife. But have you
ever dwelt on verses 17 and 18? They read, "And Abraham
prayed to God; and God healed Abimelech and his wife and
his maids, so that they bore children. For the LORD had closed
fast all the wombs of the household of Abimelech because of
Sarah, Abraham's wife."

Here is a direct statement of God's control in matters of
conception. The household of Abimelech was suddenly barren.
We are not told how long the barrenness lasted, but we do
know who was the cause and cure of it.

Sarah: The Lord Did For Her As He Had Promised.

Let's look at the next two verses while we're with Abraham
and his wife. Chapter 21:1–2 states, "Then the LORD took note
of Sarah as He had said, and the LORD did for Sarah as He
had promised. So Sarah conceived and bore a son to Abraham
in his old age, at the appointed time of which God had spoken
to him."

What a wonderful fulfillment of prophecy — and what a
crystal clear statement by Moses of just *who* was in charge in
the events and timing of the birth of Isaac! Notice the key
phrases above: "the LORD did," and "at the appointed time."
Two truths are evident here. First, God *caused* Isaac's conception. Second, *He* did it at the time He chose. So again we see
our God presenting Himself as the One in complete command
of pregnancy, even as far as the correct timing of fertilization
is involved.

Rachel and Leah: The Fertility Bowl.

Genesis 29:31 through Genesis 30:24 is one of the most amazing Scripture passages concerning God's causal relationship to conception. We meet Rachel and Leah, Jacob's wives, and discover that they are obviously not like most modern women in their attitudes toward childbearing and family size. Rather than quote the whole passage here, let's examine it, using the framework of a multi-year football game: The Fertility Bowl. The two teams are known by their star players, Leah and Rachel.

First Quarter

- First play — God opens Leah's womb. Result: Reuben
- Second play — The same play. Result: Simeon
- Third play — Once again. Result: Levi
- Fourth play — the final play of the drive. Result: Judah

Second Quarter

After dominating the opening quarter, Leah has no more children, so Rachel takes over on offense. We must point out a very innovative aspect of this game — both teams have the same quarterback — Jacob! Most unusual. Well, Rachel's demand in the huddle is, "Give me children, or else I die." Rachel really wants to get in the game. She also thinks that on this team the quarterback calls the plays, but Jacob knows full well it is the Coach who does and responds to her, "Am I in place of God, who has withheld from you the fruit of the womb?"

Now we see an unprecedented move: the first substitution. Rachel benches herself and sends in Bilhah—totally without the Coach's endorsement.

- First play with Bilhah—Result: Dan
- Second play—Result: Naphtali

Leah sees the fruitfulness of substitution and sends in Zilpah for herself.

- First play with Zilpah—Result: Gad
- Second play—Result: Asher

The first half comes to an end and so do Bilhah's and Zilpah's usefulness as players. During half-time players indulge in some trading of mandrakes, considered a sort of Old Testament fertility steroid, and Leah finds herself a "starter" once again.

Third Quarter

- First play with Leah back—Result: Issachar
- Second play—Result: Zebulun
- Third play—Result: Dinah

Fourth Quarter

Rachel is not to be outdone and in the closing minutes of the Bowl has a real "winner" in Joseph (who later becomes the first player to wear a multi-colored jersey before being traded to the farm team in Egypt). The final score is Leah 7, Rachel 2 (the second being Benjamin).

Let's watch an instant replay of God's part in the story of Rachel and Leah. Please study carefully the following references (all from the book of Genesis, so only chapter and verse are given):

- "He opened her womb." (29:31)
- "He has therefore given me this son also." (29:33)
- "Am I in the place of God, who has withheld children from you?" (30:2)
- "God has vindicated me . . . and has given me a son." (30:6)
- "And God gave heed to Leah and she conceived." (30:17)
- "And God gave heed to her and opened her womb." (30:22)

These inspired examples again show God's total control over the events of birth. He "opened" and He "withheld." It is imperative that we grasp the significance of what God is teaching about human origins here.

Moses: God Conceives and Brings Forth.

What did Moses himself believe about conception? How would Moses have answered our chapter's question: Where do babies come from? In Numbers 11:12 the beleaguered leader asks God a rhetorical question, "Was it I who conceived all these people? Was it I who brought them forth?"

Moses understood very well that God had brought forth the nation of Israel — both spiritually *and* physically.

Moses Again: The Lord Makes You Abound.

The final quote from the Pentateuch comes from the well known blessing/cursing chapter, Deuteronomy 28. In this pas-

sage God tells Israel just how good things will be if they will
be obedient and just how horrible life will become if they are
not. Speaking through Moses, in the eleventh verse God says,
"And the LORD will make you abound in prosperity, in the
offspring of your body."

One part of the many-faceted blessing Israel could have
enjoyed was reproductive fruitfulness. Earlier, in verse 4 God
says that the children they would be given would be blessed —
again, only if they lived according to His laws. The important
words of this verse are "the LORD will." It is God who gives
offspring.

Ruth: The Lord Enables You to Conceive.

Let us now look at the beautiful book of Ruth. Ruth 4:13
states, "So Boaz took Ruth, and she became his wife, and he
went in to her. And the LORD enabled her to conceive, and she
gave birth to a son."

So Obed was born, not as a result of a chance fertilization
at the proper time of some month, but because and only because God "enabled" it. (By the way, it would be equally accurate both biologically and theologically for each of us to
place our own name in the place of "Obed" in the previous
sentence.) This new son may have looked like any other little
bundle of Jewish joy, but he was to be King David's grandpa!
Who knows what great place in God's plans a future little one,
which He could give to you or us, might play?

Samuel: The Lord Closed and the Lord Opened.

The birth of Samuel is yet another illustration of the reality of
who is the actual source of all people's lives. Our interest in
the story begins at 1 Samuel 1:6, which says, "Her rival, how-

ever, would provoke her bitterly to irritate her, because the LORD had closed her womb."

God did not say that Hannah was barren because she had a tipped uterus, blocked Fallopian tubes, endometriosis, or irregular periods. The Great Physician proclaims quite matter-of-factly His diagnosis of the cause of the barrenness. He had closed her womb; i.e., He was not giving conception. (Sarah's situation is mirrored here — her "barrenness" was only temporary, God waiting for the perfect time to cause conception.) But after a visit with Eli the outlook improves tremendously! In 1 Samuel 1:19 we read, "And Elkanah had relations with Hannah his wife, and the LORD remembered her. And it came about in due time, after Hannah had conceived, that she gave birth to a son."

What do we learn from this? Simply that Elkanah and Hannah had Samuel because God Himself accomplished it, according to His will. But we are not finished with the story — it gets even better! We know that Samuel was given to the Lord by Hannah, who had wanted a child so desperately. We also know that God rewards His people for giving Him their most treasured possessions. So what was God's reward to Hannah for "returning" Samuel? First Samuel 2:20-21 tells us, "Then Eli would bless Elkanah and his wife and say, 'May the LORD give you children from this woman in place of the one she dedicated to the LORD.' And they went to their own home. And the LORD visited Hannah; and she conceived and gave birth to three sons and two daughters."

The text does not indicate Hannah's response, but do you think she was disappointed? Here we see a case in which God gave five children, and thought it a reward! Ask yourself, how would you feel if God rewarded you with five? A lot of work?

Certainly. A lot of blessing? We know it is — once you learn how to capitalize on it!

David: God Planned You.

Some of you are sitting out there anticipating our next passage — Psalm 139. There could not be a more amazing section of Scripture than this which chronicles so wonderfully the Divine beginning of each of our lives. In verses 13 through 16 David says:

> For Thou didst form my inward parts;
> Thou didst weave me in my mother's womb.
> I will give thanks to Thee, for I am fearfully and
> wonderfully made;
> Wonderful are Thy works,
> And my soul knows it very well.
> My frame was not hidden from Thee,
> When I was made in secret,
> And skillfully wrought in the depths of the earth.
> Thine eyes have seen my unformed substance;
> And in Thy book they were all written,
> The days that were ordained for me,
> When as yet there was not one of them.

We will not delve into an in-depth exposition of this passage, but if you meditate on it, we guarantee a great blessing.

Putting aside for the moment the question of whether babies-in-the-abstract come from God, think about where *you* in-the-concrete came from. Psalm 139 tells you that you are not a statistical product, but were *begun* — "formed," "woven," "wrought." Even the number of days you are given on the earth from conception to decomposition has been specifically chosen by God. None of us is an "accident"!

Ezekiel: God Causes Population Growth.

Another question we might ask is, "Just how did Israel (the descendants of just one man, Jacob) become such a multitude that even in Egypt the Egyptians were afraid of them?" After studying all of the passages above, we could make a very educated answer! In Ezekiel 16 God speaks directly to Israel and tells His people just how they happened to become so numerous. He says in verse seven, "I made you numerous [literally a *myriad*] like plants of the field."

God claims He is totally responsible for Israel's meteoric population growth.

Psalm 100: It Is He Who Has Made Us.

The teaching of the Old Testament may be summarized by saying that children are not simply the result of a sexual union, but a direct gift from God. The Bible certainly does not deny that there is a cause-and-effect connection between sexual intercourse and conception, but it denies that conception is inevitable, or that the parents possess the power to make it happen. In fact, Psalm 100:3 states the matter with crystal clarity: "It is He who has made us, and not we ourselves."

Saying that we parents do not possess the ability to ensure conception is actually one of the understatements of all time!

Understanding where new human beings, including you and me, come from is the groundwork for the blessings to follow.

All these Scriptural examples prove that God controls the process of fertilization; that you and I are *not* products of probability, but of His ability. God has ordained the specific starting point of every life ever lived, including any future

children He might give us or you. Yet, what about the New
Testament? Does it continue this teaching?

New Testament Examples

Elizabeth: The New Deal.

In the New Testament God's *Declaration of Independence in
Conception* continues. Now it's poor barren Elizabeth's turn to
be blessed. In Luke 1:24-25 it is written, "And after these
days Elizabeth his wife became pregnant; and she kept herself
in seclusion for five months, saying, 'This is the way the Lord
has dealt with me in the days when He looked with favor
upon me, to take away my disgrace among men.' "
    There was no question in Elizabeth's mind as to who
should get the credit for her great joy. God had "looked with
favor" on her and created John.

Luke: A Doctor's Diagnosis.

Dr. Luke submits the medical report for Elizabeth in chapter
one verse fifty-eight: "And her neighbors and her relatives
heard that the Lord had displayed His great mercy toward her;
and they were rejoicing with her."
    Luke, for all his medical training and experience, had a far
more scientifically accurate concept of origins than most of
today's scientists and doctors, for he understood perfectly that
John's life was a direct result of God's "display of great
mercy toward her."

Hebrews: The Tome of the Unknown Author.

The author of the Epistle to the Hebrews held to the same view. In chapter six verse fourteen he quotes Genesis 22:17 saying, "I will surely bless you, and I will surely multiply you." And in chapter eleven verse eleven he holds up Sarah's faith in God as the Giver of children to encourage our faith: "By faith even Sarah herself received ability to conceive, even beyond the proper time of life, since she considered Him faithful who had promised."

Jesus: Conception Without Fertilization.

This example is the finest, so we saved it for last. Here we find a very strong argument for the doctrine that *God*, not statistical probability, controls conception. We are referring to the conception of our Savior, Jesus Christ, by the Holy Spirit. This is the perfect example that God ultimately and infinitely does whatever He pleases in conception. Not only did the Father pick the exact time that His Son would come to earth ("in the fullness of times"), but the Scriptures demonstrate that God could operate even despite the total absence of an ingredient most would deem absolutely essential for fertilization.

The joyous fact is that *God* opens and closes the womb! He alone decides when and if anyone will have any (more) children. And not only does He decide, He then makes it happen. We know, based on the Scriptural evidence, that if we have any more children, it will be His choosing and doing!

≫+ ≫+ ≫+

It's exam time. Here's your question: "Where do babies come from?" (Hint: It's an open and shut case!)

Focus

In this foundational chapter we looked at a score of Biblical passages dealing directly with conception and who is responsible for it. But for space we left out nearly thirty other examples! They appear in Appendix C. Examine these questions and note any comments or insights you have.

- Do you know of any Scriptural evidence indicating that God does not control conception?

- Have you been challenged in your thinking about who controls the conception process? How so?

- How often have you seen the terms *multiply* and *blessing* linked?

- How did Elizabeth's society react to her pregnancy?

- How does the reaction of your friends or relatives influence you?

3

FOR GOD SO LOVES THE . . . KIDS!

Several years ago I cleaned carpets part-time. Besides developing an allergic reaction to shag carpet and messy pets, I learned a lot about what people thought about the kids they had and about their opinions on the prospect of having more.

Would I lose credibility if I said today children are considered an unmitigated blessing? Or that people rhapsodize about their kids when they let their hair down, forgetting the carpet cleaning man is listening? You tell me! It's still not too difficult to find an occasional family who reveres their children, but from my experience, children today are definitely esteemed a little lower than the angels. W. C. Fields, who said that any man who hated kids and dogs couldn't be all bad, is a not-too-extreme example of how Americans value children.

The Case Against Kids

I first noted this type of thinking while cleaning rugs in May
or late August. The prevailing attitude in May was "Oh no!
They'll soon be home all summer! What am I going to do?
What am I going to do?" And in August—"Soon I'll have my
days to myself again! I can't wait for school to start!" Comments of this sort were not the exception. They were the rule!

Casual observation shows us that today, parents just don't
want their children around all that much. (In fact, the true miracle of television is that everyone can be in the same room
and still not be around.)

There are some reasons behind this way of thinking. Kids
are trouble—they cost a lot to have, the new ones keep you up
half the night, and they're such inept communicators that when
they cry you often don't have a clue as to the reason. You can't
take them some places, either. I was once playing in a symphony concert and we were in one of the gorgeous slow sections in Dvorak's Eighth when a baby started to cry. After several seconds the conductor stopped us and smack dab in the
middle of everything said, "Will the person with the crying
baby please leave!" (He wasn't asking either—he was *telling!*)

A nursing newborn can be even more restricting. Babies
wreak such havoc on a woman's career that entire magazines
are now devoted to containing the damage. The havoc extends
to vacations, and, it goes without saying, sleep. Infants tend to
do what they want, when they want. They're such babies!

All the popular parenting magazines warn you that when
the children are growing up you will have to worry about both
what they *aren't* learning in school and what they *are* learning; if your boy will make the soccer team; if your girl will
need a couple of thousand dollars worth of fencing on her

teeth; who they'll be dating and what they'll be doing; their attitude toward spiritual things; and their growing independence, modulating (so the magazines tell us) into rebellion. You worry if they'll graduate from high school and then if they do, you'll worry more about what you'll use to pay for college.

The more children we have, the less things we can have. Maybe a shorter vacation, maybe no vacation, perhaps non-designer clothes, perhaps less snazzy cars—who ever heard of a nine-passenger Corvette?

Our culture has more incentive to chase after material things than any preceding it. There are so many really wonderful things to see and have and do! Trouble is, they all cost money. Double trouble is, so do kids. As the old song states, "something's gotta give." So, prompted by twenty-five billion dollars a year of mass advertising, we tend to fall into the habit of giving ourselves more *things* rather than more children. As an acid test of the truth of this statement, perform the following test. Ask ten people this question: "If you could have one million dollars or one more child, which would you choose?" (For a *really* acid test, knock the offer down to ten thousand dollars and see what happens!)

The ultimate proof that we Americans don't really like kids is evidenced by two numbers separated by a dot: 1.8. That's how many (or few) kids the average U.S. family has—not even enough to replace us. Yuppies have given way to DINKS (Dual Income, No Kids). According to the 1989 *Statistical Abstract of the United States,* we now average more TV's per household than kids, probably because TV's require no discipline, never wet the bed, and don't have to learn to drive.

Yup—the world thinks kids are too much trouble, and now many Christians are agreeing. For example, in our survey (in

Appendix B) several married Christian respondents said that their ideal number of children was less than what they had.

A Word's-Eye View of Kids

This has been our coverage of the world's attitude towards kids. Now, back for a word or two from the Word!

The Bible's most explicit statement about how much children are worth appears in Psalm 127:3-5. Solomon, the wisest man in the world, wrote this psalm. Let's read what Solomon says about children.

> Behold, children are a gift of the LORD;
> The fruit of the womb is a reward.
> Like arrows in the hand of a warrior,
> So are the children of one's youth.
> How blessed is the man whose quiver is full
> of them;
> They shall not be ashamed when they speak with
> their enemies in the gate.

We see five phrases here. By examining each of them, we can better discover God's eternal feelings about children.

Phrase One: "Behold, children are a gift of the LORD."

Do we really believe that? If children *are* a gift from God, let's for the sake of argument ask ourselves what other gift or blessing from God we would reject. Money? Would we reject great wealth if God gave it? Not likely! How about good health? Many would say that a man's good health is his most treasured possession. But *children?* Even children given by God? "That's different!" some will plead. All right, is it dif-

ferent? God states here in no-nonsense language that children
are gifts. Do we believe His Word to be true?

Cut away for a moment to the Rose Garden of the White
House. The President of the United States of America is presenting a couple with a gift of fabulous value. Scores of television cameramen and photographers are ready to capture the
recipients' reaction for millions to see. Do they accept graciously and warmly thank the President? No! They blanch and
blurt out, "Oh no — not another one of *those!* We already have
one! No way! We've decided it would be just too much trouble!" Wow, would the media have a field day with them!

How insulting to refuse a gift from anyone. How much
worse if that gift was a planned and specially prepared life
from the Creator!

Phrase Two: "The fruit of the womb is a reward."

There it is in black and white. Children are a *reward.* They are
a bonus! A promotion! A public honor bestowed by God!

"A reward? A reward for what? What have I done to deserve a reward?"

Well, here is the good news — you may be rewarded with
perhaps the greatest possible reward, a human being, just for
being God's child and being an object of His love.

"What a deal! What could be better?"

This! That the reward you are given is unique — none other
like it in the universe. Planned for you, it may even look like
you! It will eat with you, maybe even sleep with you sometimes when they are little (especially during thunderstorms!).
It comes with a guarantee — God promises that this reward will
positively be good for you (Romans 8:28)!

What a gracious God we have!

Phrase Three: "Like arrows in the hand of a warrior, so are the children of one's youth."

Our children are similar to a warrior's arrows. This is an unexpected comparison! We might have expected them to be likened to little lambs or little jewels or little balls of fire. But arrows? Instead of delving into this now, we will put it off until the final chapter. Then the reason for the analogy — and the blessing it brings — will be made plain, and you may be as excited as we are.

Phrase Four: "How blessed is the man whose quiver is full of them."

One of the things we really like to do together as a family is to go for walks at our big shopping center here in town. It's wonderfully inexpensive, and Jan and I could write doctoral dissertations in sociology just from observing the faces of the people as our herd thunders past. Sometimes there will be an elderly person or couple, and they will nod their heads and smile at us approvingly. That is heartwarming. Unfortunately, the majority of the looks we get, especially from couples more our age and younger, is one of pity or even distaste. Were these people paraphrasing the above verse, it might come out, "How unfortunate is the man . . ."

This has become the majority evangelical reaction as well.

At a dinner party with some Christian friends, someone brought up the subject of birth control. One of the women present asked Jan and me the question, "Don't some people think of you as being foolish?" We knew that she did not, but we had to answer, "Yes." Does that ever bother us? Only rarely, but even then the feeling invoked in us is not resentment or anger but frustration and sadness at how out of alignment things are. We do know and rest in the fact that God does not consider us foolish in gratefully accepting His presents, and it is His approval we desire. From studying the Scriptures we realize that He actually considers Himself to be blessing us when He gives us a child. We will see *why* later!

Now this matter of the "quiver." It originates from the Hebrew word pronounced *ash-paw.* For years I heard that the Hebrew quiver of Old Testament times held five or six arrows, and that satisfied me. It seemed to be an intelligent, if larger than average, limit. At least a lid was available for an otherwise nastily open-ended concept. Never mind that no where does God even *hint* at a limit of half a dozen.

Well, several years ago, much to my astonishment, I heard an actual archaeologist from the Middle East state matter-of-factly that the correct number of arrows was between twelve and fifteen!

The reason pictures of ancient warriors etched in stone often showed five or six arrows per quiver was for the same reason that those warriors looked all alike. It takes far more time and dexterity to show lots of arrows in a tiny etched quiver than it does to sketch the idea of "many arrows" by just a few lines. You try etching fifty warriors in stone sometime and see if you're not tempted to slim down the arrow quota!

A personal note here: I did not serve in the military and am, therefore, probably not a leading candidate for appointment to the Joint Chiefs of Staff. But even I have to admit that if I were a Jewish general in a heated battle with the Philistines, I would be much more confident if the members of my archery division each had a dozen arrows rather than just half or quarter that many.

To avoid any misunderstandings concerning the message of this book, realize that we are *not* stating that every couple must have twelve to fifteen children! Couples need only trust God to provide them with the perfect number of children for their situation. God can choose the ideal number for any couple. Let's just not base our thinking on a mythical six-child maximum. The fact here is inarguable — a man with a full quiver, i.e., *the number he is supposed to have* is described by God as "blessed"!

Phrase Five: "They shall not be ashamed when they speak with their enemies in the gate."

The obvious meaning of this phrase is that a well-armed man will do well in confrontations with his enemies. This brings to mind a recurring theme from old episodes of *Bonanza* in which the father, Ben Cartwright, would be dealing with some bad dudes in a really tough situation. At the height of tension, who should ride up but Adam, Hoss, and Little Joe. Any troubles were soon over, always favorably, and in plenty of time for a commercial. I never saw Ben ashamed in any gate when his arrows were around.

To close our discussion of Psalm 127, here is a quote from Joseph Caryl, who said in Charles Spurgeon's *Treasury of David,*

> Hence note, 'tis one of the greatest outward blessings to have a family full of dutiful children. To have many children is the next blessing to much grace. To have many children about us is better than to have much wealth about us. To have store of these olive plants (as the Psalmist calls them) round about our table is better than to have store of oil and wine upon our table. We know the worth of dead, or rather lifeless treasures, but who knows the worth of living treasures? . . . But though all things are of God, yet all

things are not alike of him: children are more of God than houses or lands.

Our next stop, Psalm 128, is close in more ways than one to Psalm 127. This is a beautiful Psalm which deals again with God's own attitude toward our having children. We are looking at verses 3 and 4, which say:

> Your wife shall be like a fruitful vine,
> Within your house,
> Your children like olive plants
> Around your table.
> Behold, for thus shall the man be blessed
> Who fears the LORD.

After reading this, the response of some may be to rush out and purchase a very small table. However, this passage should send us garage "sailing" for baby stuff! God points out to us in uplifting and very positive words that giving us kids is giving us blessings.

Did you notice that in the space of one psalm, God has completely changed His description of children? They have changed from "arrows" to "olive plants." The *Westminster Dictionary of the Bible* (p. 438) says this about the olive plant, "The olive was also a symbol of prosperity and divine blessing, of beauty and strength (see Psalm 52:8, Jeremiah 1:16, Hosea 14:6)." Now a two-year-old encased in lasagna, as Shakespeare put it, "from nave to chops," is hardly a model of beauty and strength! Patience is an important prerequisite for the blessing of children. We must wait for our "olives" to mature before all of their virtues appear.

I think it's pretty clear by now that if God gives you or me a child, He considers the child a real live *blessing!* Those people who think that children are primarily trouble and large families are to be pitied are not sitting on God's side of the blessing.

Consider this quote from *Unger's Bible Dictionary* (p. 148), "God's blessing is accompanied with that virtue which renders His blessing effectual and which is expressed by it." In other words, God sees to it that His blessings are just that—in this case not happenstance births, but planned incidents of goodness.

Here is an important point—not only does God provide children as a blessing, He *withholds* them as a punishment. Evidence of this is found in the account of Abimelech, Abraham, and Sarah which we looked at in the last chapter. The teaching is found also in Hosea 9. In this section the prophet is listing the sins of Ephraim. One punishment God promised is pronounced in verse 11, "As for Ephraim, their glory will fly away like a bird—No birth, no pregnancy, and no conception!"

The Second Gap Theory

Now some may wonder why we don't find more of this in the New Testament if it is so important for us today. That questioning is at the heart of the Second Gap Theory. Just as the First Gap Theory postulates a vast time-gap between the first two verses of the Bible, this Second Gap imagines an equally huge gap, not of time, but purpose, between the Old and New Testaments. This gap is not taught in theology books, but in statements like, "But that's the *Old* Testament!"

We believe both gaps to be false. The idea is like saying that the Old Testament was the rough draft, but the New is the final copy. Now there *are* significant differences between Testaments and sound hermeneutics demands that we observe those differences. The trouble is that we tend to conveniently dismiss things in the Old Testament that make us uncomfortable or squeamish as being too Law-ish and therefore non-applicable.

The New Testament succinctly explains how we are to view and use the Old Testament. The writer to the Hebrews says in Hebrews 4:12, "For the word of God is living and active and sharper than any two-edged sword, and piercing as far as the division of soul and spirit, of both joints and marrow, and able to judge the thoughts and intentions of the heart." Paul, in 2 Timothy 3:16-17 says, "All Scripture is inspired by God and profitable for teaching, for reproof, for correction, for training in righteousness; that the man of God may be adequate, equipped for every good work." The words of importance used in Hebrews and 2 Timothy are *"All Scripture"* and *"the word of God."* Both are talking about the Old Testament, since that's all the Scripture there was at the time those passages were written. We can read the New Testament into these passages—and there is no question as to the New Testament's divine inspiration—but we are certainly reading it in here. Those passages are saying that the *Old* Testament is God-breathed, inspired by God, and profitable for teaching, reproof, correction, and training in righteousness.

The position of the New Testament on the use of the Old is very clear. In Hebrews the Old Testament is alive. It is active, it pierces and judges us. In 2 Timothy *all* of the Old Testament is declared profitable, containing everything to make us adequate and able to do every good work.

At least two New Testament passages deal with the subject of children. In Titus 2:4 Paul charges older women with the task of training younger women. He lists several areas of training, ". . . that they may encourage the young women to love their husbands, to love their children."

It seems almost silly to bring this up, but if the young women are to be taught to love their children, they *must have some* to love! Paul's assumption that Christian marriage should as a matter of course yield children is seen in his instruction on the care of widows in 1 Timothy 5:14, "Therefore, I want younger widows to get married, bear children, keep house, and give the enemy no occasion for reproach."

This passage stands very clearly against planned barrenness. A lifestyle free of children is not an available option for the young remarried widow. Nor is there any reason to suppose that the women Paul urges to "love their children" in the Titus passage are being encouraged to avoid childbearing!

Is God changeless? Does He still hate disobedience as always? Does He still love His children as always? Does He still consider our offspring blessings and rewards from Him? Well, what *does* the New Testament teach about God's attitude toward His little creations?

Jesus Loves the Little Children

In the gospel of Mark we see Jesus actually *indignant* over the treatment His little gifts were getting at the hands of His own disciples. We read in 10:13-16:

> And they were bringing children to Him so that He might touch them; and the disciples rebuked them. But when Jesus saw this, He was indignant and said to them, "Permit the children to come to Me; do not hinder them; for the kingdom of God belongs to such as these. Truly I say to you, whoever does not receive the kingdom of God like a child

shall not enter it at all." And He took them in His arms and began blessing them.

Jesus acted more upset when the disciples shooed children out of His adult society than when the chief priests and Pharisees turned Him over to be crucified! The Greek word expressing His reaction, translated "indignant" here, literally means "very grieved." The Savior's response shows very clearly His attitude toward the children He has given.

Christ is not only concerned that children should be allowed to come to Him, but that we should actively *welcome* them in His Name. We see this illustrated in Matthew 18:1-6:

> At that time the disciples came to Jesus, saying, "Who then is greatest in the kingdom of heaven?" And He called a child to Himself and stood him in their midst, and said, "Truly I say to you, unless you are converted and become like children, you shall not enter the kingdom of heaven. Whoever then humbles himself as this child, he is the greatest in the kingdom of heaven. And whoever receives one such child in My name receives Me; but whoever causes one of these little ones who believe in Me to stumble, it is better for him that a heavy millstone be hung around his neck, and that he be drowned in the depth of the sea."

Here is a teaching that we parents must keep in focus constantly—no matter how many children God entrusts to us, they are never totally ours; they are ever His. In Ezekiel 16:20 God says to the Jews, "Moreover, you took your sons and daughters whom you had borne to Me. . . ." Two chapters later God says, "Behold, all souls are Mine; the soul of the father as well as the soul of the son is Mine" (18:4). Our children are a stewardship entrusted to us by the God who planned, designed, and began them. What a responsibility. What an honor!

➤➤   ➤➤   ➤➤

In the first chapter we saw that God alone causes (or withholds) conception. Now, in this chapter we have seen that God not only values children, but He considers He is doing us a favor in gracing us with them.

True, realizing and applying these truths is not always easy or automatic. Here's a word from Jan on that subject.

I used to wonder how the psalmists could say that we are blessed by having a quiver full of children or that a man who fears the Lord will be blessed with a fruitful wife and many "olive plants" around his table. Didn't they ever have to begin spanking a two-year-old, only to find out he had messy diapers? Didn't their children ever feel left out or misunderstood, making sure that everyone else in the family knew it as well? Didn't their central air unit ever break down in mid-summer when their wives were nine-plus months pregnant? Wasn't it a constant struggle for them to teach their children to spiritually discern evil rather than experience it and make choices?

But wait! These men were writing under the inspiration of God. They are right! Children are a blessing. They are a reward—a compensation, a benefit. Those who have a quiver and a table full are happy, fortunate, and to be envied by the rest of the world.

Ah-ha! That's the key! Our world is being deceived by its ruler, Satan, into thinking that children are a threat or at best a horrible inconvenience. Even the church is being led astray by those who adulterate or handle dishonestly the Word of God (see 2 Corinthians 4:2-4).

We need to believe God. If He says children are a blessing and we disagree, we must change and begin seeing them from His point of view. Will it be easy? Experience tells us 'no.' Will we be blessed (happy, fortunate, enviable, benefited) if we persist in faith? Yes — as you will see in the rest of this book. We will be blessed according to God's standards, not the world's — a lifelong blessing that far surpasses anything the world has to offer.

We need to refocus our vision to see as God sees. We need to see the results of training a two-year-old to respond immediately to his parents — bringing delight and comfort to us as parents and amazement and awe to friends and relatives. (He won't always have messy diapers either!) We need to have our children come to *us* with their hurt feelings and anxieties, rather than other friends, as we reach out to them in unconditional love. We need to learn to be grateful that we ever had central air at all and trust God to provide to fix it. We need to grow closer as a family as we discern from God's principles what is right and wrong.

May God constantly remind us to keep our eyes on Him and not on ourselves or the world. Then we will clearly see what a blessing children are.

Focus

- Conduct your own acid survey from page 27. Ask several couples of childbearing age (or strangers if you're bold) the question: "If you could have either one million dollars or another baby, which would you choose?" If they take the money and run, knock the offer down to ten thousand dollars. How about ten dollars? Ask why for either answer. Why would (or did) some people choose the money? If you get a

negative reaction, ask "How much would you have to be paid
to have another baby?"

- Review the Caryl quote on page 32. How does Mr. Caryl's
  attitude differ from the world's? Does it differ from the
  church's?

- In what areas besides receiving children do (or should) Christians and the world have differing views?

4

GUESS WHO'S
NOT COMING TO DINNER

A new chapter and a new focus. In chapter one we discovered whether we were more like Jake or more like Jennifer. Chapter two showed where babies come from. Chapter three demonstrated that God is blessing us in giving us children.

Now in this chapter we want to be imaginative. Imagine yourself with, say, eight children. What do you think your life would be like? Maybe a better question would be, what was your emotional response to imagining life with eight children?

Many acquaintances, who know how many children we have, have at one time or another said or intimated, "You must be crazy!" Was that *your* first reaction too?

You might have thought that a family with eight children will be as below average in social and intellectual development as it is above average in size. If so, you are in extremely learned company! What follows are newspaper excerpts, relating the findings of some sociologists, presented at the meeting

of the 1985 American Association for the Advancement of
Science (AAAS):

> Los Angeles (AP) — Children of small families have higher
> IQs and complete more years of schooling than do children
> of large families, even when family income is taken into
> account, scientists said Monday.
>
> One researcher noted that the surprising nationwide upturn
> of SAT scores beginning in 1980 corresponds closely to the
> decrease in family size during the 1960s and 1970s, when
> children now taking the Scholastic Aptitude Test were born.
>
> The researcher, Robert Zajonc of the University of Michi-
> gan, predicted scores would continue to climb until the year
> 2000, when the children of today's larger families will begin
> to show another decline in scores.
>
> He was one of a panel of researchers who discussed their
> research at the annual meeting of the American Association
> for the Advancement of Science.
>
> Zajonc said his research indicates that the greater the num-
> ber of children in a family and the shorter the spacing be-
> tween them, the less their intellectual maturity.
>
> Zajonc cautioned that it would be unwise to base family
> planning decisions on his research. . . .
>
> "The advantages of coming from a small family are gigan-
> tic — by that I mean two or three children," she [Judith Blake
> of UCLA] said.
>
> Her research clearly indicates a difference between families of
> two or three children and families of six or eight children, she
> said. It does not as clearly show, for example, whether having
> two children might be better than having three, she said.
>
> James Higgins, of Michigan State University, disagreed
> somewhat with these findings, arguing that the parents of

large families tend to have low IQs and that therefore the children's IQs are merely a reflection of their parents' and are not related to the size of their families. (*Omaha World Herald,* [May 28, 1985])

Now that hurts, Dr. Higgins! The first time I read the article I was shocked—then I laughed! I had to wonder though, was there any truth to this? Even if it was true, that would not be grounds to "play God," of course, but still we wondered. How could we check out this theory? Then came the answer—history.

What If . . .

We are going to engage in a bit of "what if?" in this chapter. We all know what that means; what if Muhammed Ali had fought Joe Lewis? What if Germany had developed the atomic bomb before we did in World War II? What if Luther and Zwingli had focused on their fourteen points of agreement instead of the one point of disagreement at the Marburg in 1529? What if you had ninety-seven million dollars?

Our grand and glorious "what if?" is this: What if everyone throughout history had held to the current viewpoint that two children is enough? How would history have been different?

We pose this question, because so many Christians today believe that it is perfectly normal and, according to our survey, even *wise* to have small families. We may not believe in a natural maximum allotment of, say, 500 IQ points per family, so that the more children we have, the less points each child gets, but we may entertain other equally fanciful ideas. Maybe we feel that children will not be able to express creativity or leadership in a large family as well as would be possible in a small family. The AAAS sociologists quoted earlier certainly think *something* is deleterious in the large family setting.

This chapter is a historical mini-survey, specifically focusing on the gaping holes that would be left in three unrelated fields if the parents of yesteryear had operated under the present value system.

As an aside, we are not saying that large families *guarantee* creativity, leadership, or spirituality, since the rule of the day used to be larger families and not everyone was a Bach. What we will be pointing out is that big families are not detrimental to the formation of talent, opportunity, or ministry, and they can actually help nuture many positive areas and aspects of children's lives.

The Dinner Party

If there is one point of theology upon which all believers can agree, it must be that they like to get together to eat! Given this propensity for food, let's suppose that you decide to give a dinner party for some of the greats of history. In fact, you have scheduled three different parties. There is only one stipulation on the invitations.

The average family now has fewer than two children, so we will be very generous and allow these oldsters a three child cut off! Based on this limit, should we expect many no-shows for the parties? Let's see what the family size concepts and controls of today would have done to the pages of history. In other words, guess who's not coming to dinner! Have a look on the next page at the invitations that you're sending out.

> ## YOU ARE MOST CORDIALLY INVITED TO A DINNER PARTY TO BE HELD AT OUR HOME ON FRIDAY EVENING AT 8:00.
>
> Due to cultural considerations, we are requesting that only first-, second-, or third-born persons be in attendance.
>
> ## R.S.V.P.

Unsung Heroes—A Party Without Music

Your first group of invitations goes out—to the great musicians of history. This should be a safe group to invite, since it is commonly held that creativity and artistic expression flower more fully in smaller family environments.

Music is a favorite interest of ours, and in the Hess home serious music is heard much of the day. We also enjoy listening to Christian radio and singing together. Jan has become quite a connoisseur of music herself. She can distinguish Bach from Vivaldi, Beethoven from Brahms, Tchaikovsky from Rimsky-Korsakov, and Bernstein from Copland. It was fun to hear then seven-year-old Adam walking around the house robustly vocalizing "In the Hall of the Mountain King" or picking out "Pomp and Circumstance" on the piano, or to hear Staci, our then eleven-year-old, humming "The Great Gate of Kiev" from *Pictures at an Exhibition.*

I thought it would be instructive and interesting to find out what would have happened in the world of music had the families of the great composers and performers adopted the same philosophy that the world and much of the church have today. I was quite surprised. Your invitations have been sent, and the RSVP's are returning. Following is a list of some composers who would not be in attendance if their parents had been the "normal" parents of today.

To begin, if you commissioned one hundred musicologists to come up with the four greatest composers in the history of music, you would be likely to get a consensus list of Bach, Beethoven, Brahms, and Mozart. Tough luck. Only Johannes Brahms (1833-1897) would show up at your party. You see, Johann Sebastian Bach (1685-1750) was eighth in his family. Wolfgang Amadeus Mozart (1756-1791) was the last of seven! Beethoven should *never* have been allowed to be born; his family story is amazing. Ludwig's father had contracted syphilis and his mother tuberculosis. Their first child was born blind, baby number two died, deafness was the lot of number three, the fourth child had his mother's illness. That's enough to make most people quit. It wasn't enough in this case, for the fifth child was Ludwig van Beethoven (1770-1827). The next time you are singing "Joyful, Joyful, We Adore Thee" in your hymnal (he wrote the music, not those words), be grateful the elder Beethovens had Ludwig.

The dinner party is already a disappointment, but it is going to get much worse. There will be many other no-shows for the evening. Other absentees would include:

- German composer Robert Schumann (1810-1856) was the last of five.

- German opera composer Richard Wagner (1813-1883) was the last of nine.

- French composer Jacques Offenbach (1819-1880), the man who gave us the "Can-Can," was the seventh of ten.

- Czech Bedrich Smetana (1824-1884) was number eleven of eighteen!

- Many have heard "Pictures at an Exhibition," written by the Russian composer Modest (accent on the second syllable) Mussorgsky (1839-1881), but few know he was also the eleventh of eighteen.

- Not only do you lose another guest, but Norway loses her greatest composer, Edvard Grieg (1843-1907). Edvard's parents knew they could "afjord" him, even though he was fourth of five.

- Lovers of melodious music will be saddened to lose Frenchman Gabriel Faure (1845-1924) who was the last of six children.

- Austrian Hugo Wolf (1860-1903) was fourth of eight.

- Next in this Missing Musicians list is one who is considered by many to have been the greatest Italian tenor ever. He was the eighteenth of twenty-one children. The fact that the first seventeen died at or very near childbirth only augments the wonder of Enrico Caruso's birth (1873-1921). By the way, according to a biographer of Caruso's life, there was only one girl in all twenty-one births!

- Many of today's piano virtuosi would be left high and dry as William Steinway (yes, *that* Steinway) was the seventh of seven children.

- Your last empty chair should have been filled by America's great composer Aaron Copland, born in 1900 the last of five children.

Your friends who are sitting at the table waiting to meet the great musicians you invited are not likely to be overly impressed, as the guests not present represent an enormous body of great music. And this was only a partial listing. But before we are through with the musicians, here is a list of composers who were first, second, or third born, but came from larger families than are thought proper for artists' achievement today. Again, this is far from an exhaustive list. Here are a few:

- Claudio Monteverdi (1567-1643); one of five bambinos.

- Alessandro Scarlatti (1660-1725); also one of five.

- Franz Joseph Haydn (1732-1809); Austrian, one of seventeen.

- Franz Schubert (1797-1828); another Austrian, one of fourteen.

- Anton Bruckner (1824-1896); this German composer was one of eleven.

- Gustav Mahler (1860-1911); Austrian, and our favorite symphonist, one of eleven.

- Claude Debussy (1862-1918); obviously French, one of five.

- Pablo Casals (1876-1973); Spanish cellist and composer, he was one of eleven children.

The next time you listen to *The Messiah* by George Frederick Handel (1685-1759), say "Hallelujah" because God didn't consider George's sixty-three year old dad too old to father a son. That was his age when one of history's greatest composers, and a man believed to have been a genuine believer, was born.

Johann Sebastian Bach is a fitting person to close this musical discussion. This man of God had prodigious musical ability. He excelled in all areas of music except the rhythm method, as he had twenty-one children. All who reached adulthood were accomplished musicians. What a blessing to the world they, like their father, have been.

The curtain comes down on your first dinner party . . .

The Bland Old Party
(History as an "Un-Presidented" Failure)

Perhaps we were just unlucky with the musicians. Let's mosey over to politics. American. Presidential.

The first dinner party turned out to be pianissimo rather than fortissimo, but out go new invitations, to all the presidents America has been led by. What a gathering that would be! You send out the same invitations as before, plus, of course you inform the media. Then you start to wonder, "Hmmm, how many of *these* men will be disqualified?"

Good question. Here we should expect to be safe though: IQ, so important to the AAAS sociologists, and leadership qualities should play some part in becoming a national leader, so you will expect the great majority of presidents to have been nurtured in smaller family environments, more like today's norm.

Let's find out how many of our great national leaders would have been missing had the couples of old been indoctrinated into the beliefs of our time. As per your invitations, we will eliminate all the presidents who were further down in their families than third born. Each president *in absentia* is listed below. The number in front of each name indicates what number president he was:

☆ 1 — George Washington (1732-1799); fifth of ten — a bad start.

☆ 9 — William Henry Harrison (1773-1841); last of seven.

☆ 10 — John Tyler (1790-1862); sixth of eight.

☆ 12 — Zachary Taylor (1784-1850); sixth of eight.

☆ 14 — Franklin Pierce (1804-1869); seventh of eight.

☆ 19 — Rutherford Hayes (1822-1893); fifth of five.

☆ 20 — James Garfield (1831-1881); fifth of five.

☆ 21 — Chester Alan Arthur (1829-1886); fifth of nine.

☆ 22 — Grover Cleveland (1837-1908); fifth of nine.

☆ 23 — Benjamin Harrison (1833-1901); fifth of thirteen.

☆ 24 — Grover Cleveland again.

☆ 25 — William McKinley (1843-1901); seventh of nine.

☆ 27 — William Howard Taft (1857-1930); seventh of ten.

Your second dinner gathering is going to have a 32 percent absentee rate! A landslide defeat. Your grand old party may be in danger of impeachment!

Here is a question for historical trivia buffs: Of the thirty-nine men who have been president, how many enjoyed the gigantic advantage of being an only child?

Only one — Gerald R. Ford.

Like the second list in the music section, here is a list of other presidents who came from families larger than our generous average of three children. This is the much more valuable list, since it is not *where* in the family one comes, but the overall *size* of the family that some are now saying determines intelligence and ability. The following group of presidents were first-, second-, or third-borns raised in large families:

☆ 3 — Thomas Jefferson (1743-1826); ten children.

☆ 4 — James Madison (1751-1836); twelve children.

☆ 5 — James Monroe (1758-1831); five children.

☆ 6 — John Quincy Adams (1767-1848); five children.

☆ 8 — Martin Van Buren (1782-1862); five children.

☆ 11 — James Polk (1795-1849); ten children.

☆ 13 — Millard Fillmore (1800-1874); nine children.

☆ 15 — James Buchanan (1791-1868); eleven children.

☆ 18 — Ulysses S. Grant (1822-1885); six children.

☆ 26 — Theodore Roosevelt (1858-1919); four children.

☆ 28 — Woodrow Wilson (1856-1924); four children.

☆ 29 — Warren G. Harding (1865-1923); eight children.

☆ 34 — Dwight Eisenhower (1890-1969); seven children.

☆ 35 — John F. Kennedy (1917-1963); nine children.

☆ 36 — Lyndon B. Johnson (1908-1973); five children.

☆ 37 — Richard Nixon (1913-); five children.

☆ 39 — Jimmy Carter (1924-); four children.

☆ 41 — George Bush (1924-); five children.

In all, thirty of the thirty-nine presidents (Grover Cleveland was President twice but counts only once) came from families larger (most *much* larger) than the average family of today. That is a whopping 76 percent, or three out of every four presidents. Far from being a deterrent, it appears large families are beneficial in fostering leadership characteristics.

Maybe the most interesting statistic is the average number of children in the families into which the presidents were born. The thirty-nine families had 246 children, an amazing average of *6.3* children per family. That is 350 percent larger than the average family of today.

In our present day we are advised to have few children, so that they can be individually molded for their maximum achievement. Upon first hearing, this does sound logical, but the advice breaks down in the face of hard evidence. Large families provide a fertile ground for success. They obviously have in the past, and we must believe that particularly under God's guidance they certainly can in the future.

Backtracking, we have seen that many of the great creative men of music would not have existed if today's self-determinative attitudes had prevailed back through history. Now we have seen similarly how many of our country's presidents would never have been born if their parents believed and practiced what most of modern society does.

One more historical question: how many presidents themselves had large families? As a reminder, we are allowing a four-child family as our starting point. Of the thirty-nine presidents, what percentage would you guess had larger than average families? Fifty-three percent—twenty of the thirty-nine. That is a much greater percentage than currently seen in society, as evidenced by the findings of our survey. Here is the list:

☆ 2—John Adams had five.

☆ 3—Thomas Jefferson had six.

☆ 6—John Quincy Adams had four.

☆ 8—Martin Van Buren had four.

☆ 9—William Henry Harrison had ten.

☆10—John Tyler presided over the largest family—fifteen!

☆12—Zachary Taylor had six.

☆ 13 — Millard Fillmore had thirteen.

☆ 16 — Abraham Lincoln had four.

☆ 17 — Andrew Johnson had five.

☆ 18 — Ulysses S. Grant had four.

☆ 19 — Rutherford B. Hayes had eight.

☆ 20 — James Garfield had seven.

☆ 22 & 24 — Grover Cleveland had seven.

☆ 26 — Theodore Roosevelt had six.

☆ 32 — Franklin D. Roosevelt had six.

☆ 38 — Gerald R. Ford has four.

☆ 39 — Jimmy Carter has four.

☆ 40 — Ronald Reagan has four.

☆ 41 — George Bush has five.

It is worth noting that six of the presidents who were reared in small families had large ones of their own.

It is our sad lot to point out that you are 0-for-2 in successful dinner parties. The natural response might be, "Well, who cares about a lot of ancient, long-haired, dead musicians! Most of 'em were pretty rascally characters anyway." Or, "Why use power-hungry politicos as examples for us to follow?"

Fine. If that's the way it is, we are forced to unleash *the* list.

Following is a list of men and women of God; men and women who would not have lived if their parents were as enamored by the world's family planning philosophy as our society tends to be. Our rich Christian heritage would be minus many of the preachers, missionaries, writers, leaders, etc. who have been used by God so greatly in past years. (We might add that this is your final try for a successful dinner party!)

Amazing Disgrace — Your Last Party

Before listing the names, I must say it was surprisingly difficult, even in the library of a large Christian college with thousands of biographical volumes, to be able to pinpoint how many children a famous believer grew up with. If that information was available, sometimes there was no way to determine if the person was the first- or fifteenth-born. Therefore, this list must be regarded as more incomplete than even the list of great musicians was. It is only a sampling.

It would be wonderful to eulogize these great saints, but I hope you are familiar with the majority of these mighty folks of real history, so only their names will be given. The alphabetical list follows:

✝ St. Augustine — fourth of four.

✝ Henry Ward Beecher — eighth.

✝ Dietrich Bonhoffer — eighth.

✝ David Brainerd — from a family of nine.

✝ William Jennings Bryan — fourth of nine.

✝ Oswald Chambers — fourth of nine.

✝ Sylvanus Crosby, paternal grandfather of Fanny Crosby — nineteenth of nineteen!

✝ Jonathan Edwards — eleventh of eleven.

✝ Charles Finney — seventh.

✝ Oliver B. Greene — sixth.

✝ Charles Hodge — fifth.

✝ David Livingstone — from a family of five.

✝ Dwight L. Moody — sixth of eight.

✝ Andrew Murray — at least fourth.

✝ Nate Saint — seventh of eight.

✝ C. I. Scofield — from a family of seven.

✝ A. B. Simpson — fourth of nine.

✝ J. Oswald Smith — first of ten.

✝ Corrie ten Boom — fifth.

✝ Cameron Townsend — fifth of six.

✝ Cornelius Van Til — sixth of eight.

✝ Ulrich Zwingli — third of ten.

Parents, think what might have happened (and what might *not* have happened) had the Townsends said, "Four's enough for us, thank you!," or the Moodys quit after only five, or the Edwards given up after ten girls!

There is another family to mention. They are the Wesleys. The family story begins with John and Charles' maternal grandparents, who were mildly productive. Susanna, John and Charles' mother, was their last child. As to exactly what number she was in the family, her father, in talking to another family member, said she was either "The last of two dozen or a quarter of a hundred." Fabulous! That's like questioning a Hebrew warrior on just how many arrows he has and finding out it's either twenty-four or twenty-five. He's not sure, but he knows he's ready for anything! Well, John and Charles were arrows from a much smaller quiver—only nineteen, though only nine reached adulthood. Susanna had to go through fourteen pregnancies before she got John, and then number seventeen was Charles, writer of some 6,000 hymns. Some gifts are worth waiting for.

Ladies, if you think you could not handle even four children, Jan would encourage you to read about Susanna Wesley's life. She not only got everything done, she also had time to spend individually with each of her children. She stands as an example to modern women of how God can help you organize your life, and how mightily He can use you once you have!

This third dinner party will also be marked as much by the absences as by those present.

This chapter would not be complete without a brief reflection on the importance to Biblical history of these men:

- Judah—fourth born.

- Joseph—twelfth born.

- Solomon—who knows?

Our "What if?" takes on additional importance if extended to two people; what if Jesse had stopped after seven sons—Israel would have missed its second king, and my Bible would have pages 434—510 blank. The Psalms would be gone. And what if Jacob had stopped after eleven sons? He would have missed Benjamin and we would be missing something too—like Romans, 1 Corinthians, 2 Corinthians, Galatians, Ephesians, Philippians, Colossians, 1 Thessalonians, 2 Thessalonians, 1 Timothy, 2 Timothy, Titus, and Philemon (Hebrews, anyone?), all written by the Apostle Paul, a descendant of *thirteenth-born* Benjamin.

Then there is our Savior. In Matthew 13:55-56, we are given a clue as to the size of the family in which Jesus was reared: "Is not this the carpenter's son? Is not His mother called Mary, and His brothers, James and Joseph and Simon and Judas? And His sisters, are they not all with us?"

If you would like to have a family that would be in some way like the family in which the Lord was raised, try starting off with at least seven children!

➤+   ➤+   ➤+

One purpose of this chapter has been to show what the world would have missed given present birth-control practices. Scores of different disciplines such as art, business, exploration, science, sports, and more would yield similar lists, for there would be many names in each area. The fact is that many of history's "greats" have either been born "down the line" or have been part of families whose sizes make many modern families pale in comparison—and in complexion.

A second purpose of this chapter has been to provide positive encouragement from history's pages that we would do well to give God control over how many children we have. He may then give you a J. S. Bach, a George Washington, or even a Moody—though other blessings may arrive first. We cannot see thirty seconds ahead in our lives, but God sees the end from the beginning and promises, "For I know the plans that I have for you," declares the LORD, "plans for welfare and not for calamity to give you a future and a hope" (Jeremiah 29:11).

Those plans most certainly include the children He wants to give us.

Can we trust Him as people of the past did, to their benefit and ours?

Focus

- Who would you add to our list of musicians and Christian leaders who would have missed the dinner parties? (Please send your findings to us! We'd like to compile a huge listing from many areas of life. Letters sent to our publisher Wolgemuth & Hyatt will be forwarded to us.)

- Do you think the families in which the chapter's examples were born into would have had fewer children if they could have? Why or why not?

5

THE TRIBE
OF THE ABLESSITES

I n the last chapter we dug into some interesting historical facts. We will continue in this intellectual vein by starting off with a Bible quiz — of just one question: In which book of the Bible are the Ablessites found?

This is a toughie! If the answer doesn't pop into your head you could check your concordance. If the answer doesn't pop out of your concordance, it's a very good thing, because we formulated this term ourselves. The "Ablessites" do not exist — by that name. By other names, they are quite common. If you know where to look, you can find them throughout the Bible and throughout our congregations today. We will be learning more about them in a minute.

"I Can't Faith It!"

Right now, let's think for a bit about the subject of blessings. How does a person get a blessing? Does it just randomly fall on him? Is faith involved at all? When people see a blessing coming, do they ever try to duck? If so, why?

We think it's pretty clear that many people are fleeing the kinds of blessings talked about in this book. We even have an explanation of sorts for why this is so. Let us tell you a story and see if you agree.

John is in love with Becky, a sweet and beautiful girl. Trouble is, so is Big Bad Bubba. "You come near Becky and I'm gonna break your face," Bubba informs John. Now John, out of fear of Bubba, finds himself avoiding Becky; although, left to himself he would very much like to be near her.

Becky would be a blessing to John. But something has come between them — Bubba's threats. The more Bubba menaces, the shakier John feels. John believes Bubba can beat him to a pulp, and therefore is not willing to follow his natural inclination to court Becky.

Now try thinking of John as yourself, Becky as your future baby, and Bubba as Satan. Every time you think of having a baby, Satan threatens he's going to break your face. He doesn't always do this in person, of course. His friends do it for him — the population control people, gloom-and-doom economic forecasters, hysterectomy-happy gynecologists, the women's magazines, the federal bureaucracy, and the major media! Everywhere you turn someone's telling you that if you dare to have a baby you'll be in big trouble.

The Spies Who Came in Feeling Bold

Many of us have been scared silly by the pervasive anti-baby propaganda. We can't see our way clear to collecting God's blessing because the world's threats frighten us. But that's how it has always been. Consider Numbers 13:1-2, 25-30:

> Then the LORD spoke to Moses saying, "Send out for your-self men so that they may spy out the land of Canaan, which I am going to give to the sons of Israel; you shall send a man from each of their fathers' tribes, every one a leader among them." . . . When they returned from spying out the land, at the end of forty days, they proceeded to come to Moses and Aaron and to all the congregation of the sons of Israel in the wilderness of Paran, at Kadesh; and they brought back word to them and to all the congregation and showed them the fruit of the land. Thus they told him, and said, "We went in to the land where you sent us; and it certainly does flow with milk and honey, and this is its fruit. Nevertheless, the people who live in the land are strong, and the cities are fortified and very large; and moreover, we saw the descendants of Anak there. Amalek is living in the land of the Negev and the Hittites and the Jebusites and the Amorites are living in the hill country, and the Canaanites are living by the sea and by the side of the Jordan." Then Caleb quieted the people before Moses, and said, "We should by all means go up and take possession of it, for we shall surely overcome it."

In this Bible passage we find two groups and two different exhibitions of faith. The majority (ten of the spies sent to look Canaan over) knew very well that God can be trusted; they had seen Him work themselves, doing little things like parting the Red Sea and bringing water out of solid rock. Still, they found an excuse for not exercising faith. The Bubba-ites would, they feared, break their face. The minority (Joshua and Caleb) saw the same obstacles, but showed their faith by mak-ing their decision to trust God and go ahead with His plan *in spite of* the obstacles.

Now it's time to get down to brass tacks. As a result of reading this book, many married folk are going to be faced with a *big* decision. We can trust God to be "Jehovah-jireh," the "God Who provides" for us (including our children), or we can just go it alone. The bottom-line question we all must ask is, "Can I trust God to do the best for me in controlling my family size and spacing?"

Trust or Bust

Remember what faith actually is: "Faith is the assurance of things hoped for, the conviction of things not seen" (Hebrews 11:1).

If you could see *in advance* that everything was going to work out and no obstacles needed to be overcome, you would not be exercising faith! So all the arguments about how difficult and costly and life-threatening children are just boil down to opportunities to exercise faith. No prayin', no gain.

Faith is so important to living a godly life and so essential to living a life contrary to the world and its philosophies that God says an amazing thing. A different paraphrase of Hebrews 11:6a might read, "If you do not live by faith it is *impossible* to please Me."

If we are not willing to follow God in the face of threats and worries, it is not *difficult* to please Him. It is not *hard* to please Him. It is not *real tough* to please Him. It is not even a *humdinger* to please Him. It is *impossible*—it can under no circumstances happen.

Consider this comparison. Abraham was able to believe, *entirely by faith alone,* that even if he sacrificed his son, God could raise Isaac from the dead. His faith is greater in our eyes because he had never seen or heard of God ever raising *anyone* from the dead. Why then should it be so difficult for us to believe, *entirely by faith alone,* that if we sacrifice on the altar our own plans about what size family we want, God will work His plan for our good and His glory?

Needing God

The basic attitude behind many sins is self-sufficiency, which is itself a fruit of pride. In closer-to-home terms, there can be nothing more painful than for one marriage partner to say to the other, "I don't need you." The mere thought of hearing that is almost too painful to bear; yet is it not even worse when we tell God, "I don't need to spend time with You," by neglecting to spend time with Him daily? Or by our tacit choices inform Him, "I don't want to need You; I want my life to be so smooth that Your help isn't necessary at all"?

Everyone needs God. People who live as though they know this are the most blessed people in the world.

Meet the Ablessites (but Don't Join Them!)

Now back to our imaginary Old Testament tribe, the Ablessites. Have you etymologists figured out where the name comes from? The word is made up of two parts: add "a," which is Greek for "no," to "bless" and you have it — the people who want no more blessing. No risks, no adventures, no moments trusting God.

The scary thing is that *not wanting* a blessing is enough to prevent us from obtaining it — since blessings are obtained through faith.

Paul holds up Abraham as an example of a man who had faith in God's ability to give him a child *and* make that child a blessing: "He did not waver in unbelief, but grew strong in faith, giving glory to God" (Romans 4:20).

The way to avoid membership in the Ablessite Tribe is to grow strong in faith and give the glory to God for the blessings that follow.

Trusting God with our bodies and our family size makes us stronger, like Abraham. It makes us ready to obtain even *more* blessings — and to spread them around to others. As we saw when looking at Psalm 127, it also builds up the City of God, the church. Finally, it brings glory to God. Not trusting God with our bodies and family size has ramifications too. Paul pronounced a teaching of enormous breadth to the Romans which, due to the second word, applies to us in this day and to this doctrine of blessing, ". . . and *whatever* is not from faith is sin" (Romans 14:23, emphasis added).

What If God Planned a Revival and Nobody Came?

Wouldn't it be something if God were ready to pour out a great revival on us and the only thing holding Him back was our refusal to trust Him to give us this initial blessing?

This is not a hypothetical question. Look at the last verse of the Old Testament, Malachi 4:6: "And he shall turn the hearts of the fathers to the children, and the hearts of the children to their fathers, lest I come and smite the earth with a curse."

The difference between revival and judgment may rest on whether our hearts are turned toward welcoming our present and future children. Without question, the church today does not love children.

A bad attitude towards children brings a curse. A miserly attitude towards children makes God miserly towards us. But an openhearted, generous desire for and appreciation of children as God's good gifts inclines God to trust us with many *more* good gifts — gifts we have not even seen for over 150 years now and can scarcely imagine. We will be talking about these blessings in the last chapter. But first, let's press on to deal, one by one, with the major myths that Satan has used to give us a bad attitude about children in the first place.

This chapter brings us to a point of decision. Will we exercise faith or not? Will we trust God to give us the perfect number of children at the perfect spacing? God's own testimony in the first two chapters would lead us to say, "Yes — I will trust You." Another person had to trust God. He was discussed earlier in this chapter, Abraham. Abraham had his testing place, just as we do.

A. W. Tozer's commentary from *The Pursuit of God* (pp. 30–31) sheds some light on the importance of our choice:

> If we would indeed know God in growing intimacy we must go this way of renunciation. And if we are set upon the pursuit of God, He will sooner or later bring us to this test. Abraham's testing was, at the time, not known to him as such, yet if he had taken some course other than the one he did, the whole history of the Old Testament would have been different. God would have found His man, no doubt, but the loss to Abraham would have been tragic beyond the

telling. So we will be brought one by one to the testing place, and we may never know when we are there. At that testing place there will be no dozen possible choices for us; just one and an alternative, but our whole future will be conditioned by the choice we make.

Focus

- What *Bubbas* do you face in placing your faith in God to control your family size?

- Do any couples, whom you know, live by faith in the area of their family size? Ask them how they overcame their fears and doubts.

- How does the fact that we are to live one day at a time relate to this area?

- Do you have questions which still trouble you? Please jot them down. Then, go on to the next chapter — quick!

6

THE INFAMOUS "TWENTY QUESTIONS"

F inally, the chapter we've all been waiting for! Many of
you have waded faithfully through the preceding chapters, but with nagging questions in your minds. You might be
thinking, "All right, I see all this; it seems to be correct. But
what about _____ (fill in the blank)?" A sincere question, and one which deserves an answer. Answering these
questions makes this chapter larger than any two of the others
combined.

These are the questions covered in this chapter:

- Question 1: Shouldn't I practice birth control due to overpopulation, depletion of natural resources, and food shortage?

- Question 2: But all the Christians I know use birth control!

- Question 3: Do you know how much it costs to raise a child
  these days?

- Question 4: Oh Rick and Jan, I go crazy with the kids I have now! You don't know what it would do to me to have . . . who knows how many more?

- Question 5a: What will strangers think when they see us with a large family?

- Question 5b: What will my family and friends think?

- Question 6: If I have unlimited children, how will I ever have a career?

- Question 7: You go to the doctor when you have an illness, don't you? Why not use medical expertise in this area? What's the difference?

- Question 8: Aren't we supposed to use common sense in this area of living?

- Question 9: What about the rhythm method?

- Question 10a: My doctor told me not to have any more children. Shouldn't I do what he says?

- Question 10b: What if my doctor has told me that I'm too old to safely have any more children?

- Question 10c: No, I'm serious. I have major health problems which will kill me if I have another child.

- Question 11: Didn't God have Psalms 127 and 128 written for an agricultural people? Many children would definitely be a boon in a farming situation. Most of us don't live that way today, though.

- Question 12: How can I spend quality time with a dozen kids?

- Question 13: God has led us to have "X" kids. So there!

- Question 14: Doesn't this no-birth-control philosophy mean we only have sex in order to have babies?

- Question 15: If we use birth control, isn't God free to over-rule and give us children whenever He wants, anyway?

- Question 16: Why bring children into such an evil world?

- Question 17: Doesn't this position lend itself to a particular theology?

- Question 18: I believe all this, but the thought of letting go petrifies me! What can I do?

- Question 19: What is so bad about using something as safe as the birth control methods we have today?

- Question 20: Doesn't the Bible talk about birth control at all?

Before tackling those questions, let's collect our thoughts and make sure the stage is set for this chapter. What have we learned thus far?

First, we observed that the church may not be as pro-children as we would like to think it is. Second, we discovered that conception is not governed by probability. Each conception is caused directly by God; no woman can become pregnant unless God wants her to. Third, we found out that God values His gift of children extremely highly. Fourth, we saw many famous people who came from large families. In chapter five we reminded ourselves that faith — the courage to follow God in spite of apparent obstacles — is absolutely necessary if we want to please Him, and we saw how that relates specifically to having children.

Back to your questions. We hope to have anticipated most of them in this chapter. Some questions here were expressed to Jan and me over the years by our fellow Christians. Others are questions that both of us have had to wrestle with in our own thoughts. But no matter where they come from, they need to be addressed, so here we go!

Question 1
Shouldn't I practice birth control due to overpopulation, depletion of natural resources, and food shortage?

The picture of starving children is a real and heartbreaking one. The heart of every Christian is deeply moved by such suffering. Jesus encouraged such an attitude of compassion when He taught, "Blessed are the merciful, for they shall receive mercy" (Matthew 5:7).

We can thank God for all that Christian relief agencies are doing to help in areas hit by famine and disease. But will your or my choice to avoid childbearing help those little kids on the other side of the earth — or is "overpopulation" an excuse for avoiding *real* solutions, such as giving to these agencies?

It seems odd that in the name of "helping children" we are being told not to *have* children. Yet baby-banning is definitely in. Look at this quote from *Endangered Animals,* one of the popular "Zoobooks" for children:

> The growing number of people on earth is the main cause for all of the problems shown in this book. As the human population continues to grow, there is a greater and greater demand for living space, food, lumber, minerals, and other things that must be taken from nature. Two hundred years ago, there were fewer than one billion people on earth. There was plenty of food and living space for both people and animals. Today, there are over 4 billion people on earth, and things are getting tight. In the future, if the number of humans continues to grow, there won't be any more food and room for animals.

Great stuff for a little kid to read, huh? "If only you hadn't been born, Charlie, some suffering baboon in Upper Bongo-Bongo would have had enough living space, food, lumber, and minerals."

Today babies are blamed for all kinds of political problems (and some that don't even exist). A missionary working in the Philippines remarked that this is because babies don't vote! It's far easier for politicians to persuade adults to blame "too many babies" than to get those adults to admit they are responsible for their own problems. Right now, for example, activists are trying to get the Filipinos to blame all their economic woes on overpopulation. Some of these woes are actually caused by married men who prefer to sponge off their wives' income and spend their energies on mistresses.

The idea that we would all be richer and happier if only we had less children is very popular with morally indigent, playboy types — of both sexes and all ages.

"But there *is* an overpopulation problem, isn't there?" There is if you believe pro-choicers, radical feminists, Earth-Firsters, *National Geographic,* fans of China's One-Child campaign — or Paul (*The Population Bomb*) Ehrlich.

We must be *very* careful about where we get our facts. Wrong facts lead to wrong conclusions which lead to wrong actions. Or, as Mark Twain so well stated the problem: figures don't lie, but liars figure.

We need to examine the real facts. Just how "tight" are things getting? The following lengthy excerpt is quoted by permission from a booklet entitled *How to Understand Humanism,* published by the Institute in Basic Life Principles (1983, pp. 6–7). Three questions are given and answered relative to overpopulation, natural resource shortage, and hunger.

IS THE WORLD NOW FACING THE THREAT
OF OVERPOPULATION?

Answer: No.

Those who talk about overpopulation are propagating a destructive myth. It may serve the purpose of justifying abortion, sterilization, infanticide, and euthanasia; however, it is totally contrary to the facts.

Actually, the world is comparatively empty. There are 52.5 million square miles of land area in the world, not including Antarctica.

If all the people in the world were brought together into one place, they could stand, without touching anyone else, in less than 200 square miles.

The city limits of Jacksonville, Florida contain 841 square miles. Each square mile contains 27,878,400 square feet. The total number of square feet in the city is 23,445,734,400. The world population is four and a half billion people. By allowing an average of 2.6 square feet for each person from babies to adults, every person in the world could stand shoulder to shoulder in just one-half of the city.

A further fallacy in the population explosion myth is the assumption that the greater the population, the lower the standard of living. This is not true.

Japan has a population density of 798 people per square mile, yet they have a higher per capita gross national product ($4,450) than India, which has 511 people per square mile ($140).

China has a population density of 232 persons per square mile. West Germany has 636 per square mile. The United Kingdom has 593 per square mile, and the United States has only 60 people per square mile.

IS THE WORLD RUNNING OUT OF
VITAL NATURAL RESOURCES?

Answer: No.

Projections of running out of energy or food sources are totally misleading. God gave to man the command and ability to fill up the world with people and to subdue the earth for their own needs.

Shortages of one product have always been a motivation to create a new product from existing and often overlooked resources.

Significant progress has been made in reclaiming, through irrigation, areas of land around the world which previously have been considered infertile. The vast potential of food resources in the oceans has as yet been unexplored, and many essential components of a balanced diet are now being synthesized in the laboratory.

Civilizations such as those of the Mayas and Incas were not destroyed through lack of natural resources but by moral decadence which came by rejecting Biblical truth and devoting themselves to the passions and dissipations of perverted pleasure.

Joseph was considered an expendable human being by his jealous brothers. However, God gave him the understanding which preserved his brothers during a time of famine.

How many of the 55 million babies that the world has considered expendable and has aborted in the last ten years would have been destined to discover amazing new sources for food and energy?

DOES INDIA HAVE WIDESPREAD HUNGER
BECAUSE OF LACK OF FOOD?

Answer: No.

India does not have a hunger problem because of a lack of food. It has a hunger problem because of religious beliefs which are contrary to the Word of God.

The Hindu religion teaches that people who die are reincarnated in the form of animals; thus it is against their laws and religion to kill rats, mice, cows, or other animals.

Every cow eats enough food to feed seven people, and there are two hundred million "sacred cows" in India.

If the people of India would just stop feeding these cows, they would have enough food to feed one billion, four hundred million people. That is more than one fourth of the entire world's population!

God promises adequate provision for those who serve Him and obey His laws. On the other hand, He warns that those who reject His Word will experience destructive hunger and famine.

It is for this reason that in both the Old and the New Testaments God warns us " . . . that man doth not live by bread only, but by every word that proceedeth out of the mouth of the Lord doth man live." (Deuteronomy 8:3; see Matthew 4:4)

Isn't that fascinating? How we can be fooled by popular ideas.

By the way, if the idea of having only 2.6 square feet for yourself (your allotted living space if the whole world's population had to fit in half of Jacksonville, Florida) makes you feel a tad cramped, how about an allowance *one hundred times* that large? Under those circumstances you would have an area equivalent to a family of four living in a 1,040 square foot home — certainly normal enough by our sprawling American standards and extravagant by most of the world's standards. In that case, you would have the entire world's population living in just one half of our state of Nebraska!

Now, some may want their mansions early, so how about *one thousand square feet per person?* The required area? Nebraska and Kansas. "What? The entire states of Nebraska and Kansas?" Well, to be honest, we would also need a strip about nine miles wide along the southern edge of South Dakota, just for those who like their winters a little cooler. We would still have the rest of the United States, plus Canada, Mexico, Central and South America, Europe, Africa, Asia and the Australian/South Pacific areas for food production, amusement parks, and whatever — 99.7 percent of the land area of the earth (excluding Antarctica) *all empty.*

Believe it or not, the *truth* is that there is hardly anybody home here on our planet. If U.S. agricultural methods were employed on a global scale (not to mention the huge acreage in our own country which farmers are paid not to farm) we would have to start exporting food to the Moon.

Above all, let us remember that God promises to care for His own. As Paul says in Philippians 4:13, "And my God shall supply all your needs according to His riches in glory in Christ Jesus."

The overpopulation scare is like much of the baggage left over from the sixties — fervently preached by a few, believed by many, but discarded by real leaders and those in the know. For example, these paragraphs excepted from the *Omaha World Herald* (January 22, 1984) reveals this. The article was entitled "Low Birthrate Worries West German Leaders":

> Bonn, West Germany — The security and prosperity of West Germany are becoming increasingly jeopardized by the dearth of a vital resource — children.

Since 1974, West Germans have had the world's lowest birthrate. Deaths now outpace births by more than one-third, and Chancellor Helmut Kohl's government has expressed serious concern about a dwindling native population.

A recent report to the Cabinet from several ministries showed that the impact of a steadily declining birthrate will soon pose serious consequences for national defense, education and the labor market.

The country's generous network of social services also could be eroded by the failure of a shrunken work force to generate enough revenue to support pensioners and the underprivileged.

Moreover, racial tensions may become aggravated as West Germany's 4.5 million foreigners, who have a higher birthrate, increase their share of the population.

If the birth trend continues, the native German population is expected to fall from 56.9 million today to 38.3 million in less than 50 years, according to Horst Waffenschmidt, a parliamentary secretary in Bonn's Interior Ministry.

The most immediate impact may be felt in the West German army, which requires 225,000 men each year. By next year, a shortage of eighteen-year-olds may compel the army to begin cutting the ranks of its 495,000-member standing force.

By the year 2000, the number of pupils in the nation's schools will drop by 25 percent. By the end of this decade, it is feared, about 150,000 university graduates with teaching degrees will be unemployed.

On the other hand, the government report predicts serious labor shortages in fields such as law enforcement and medicine.

Sociologists say the decade-long decline in the birthrate is the result of the birth control pill, the desire of more women to pursue careers and an urge to enjoy leisure activities unfettered by the duties of parenthood.

Unlike other European countries that have offered financial inducements of family subsidies to boost population growth, West Germany has shied away from such bounties because of the memories they evoke of the Nazi era.

In contrast to West Germany is Mongolia, which has adopted a policy of "put your money where your mommy is." The February 1985 issue of *National Geographic* said:

Births are blessed events not only for parents but also for state planners, who see population growth as crucial to national development. Couples are rewarded with subsidies for large families. A mother with ten children earns as much as a full-time factory worker.

For those interested in population issues, a must read is *The Birth Dearth*, by Ben Wattenberg. Subtitled, "What Happens When People in Free Countries Don't Have Enough Babies," the book has certainly generated some heat among the ZPG (zero population growth) types. Wattenberg, a demographer and columnist, paints a bleak picture of the West and a dark future for U.S. economics, society, and social security (people don't put money into Social Security, they put in *babies*). It is a fascinating, albeit very unsettling book.

With all apologies to Walt Disney, it's a *huge* world after all!

Question 2
But all the Christians I know use birth control!

Now, don't you feel sheepish even using this as an excuse? Of course you do. But it is an undeniable fact that folks tend to "go-with-the-flow." This unfortunate state is accurately referred to as the blind leading the blind.

As perhaps the most accurate barometer of your current family-size theology, ask yourself a question—"If most of my Christian friends had six to twelve children instead of 0-3, would I be more willing to allow God to control my reproduction?" The answer is likely "yes" for quite a few of us. Again, just following everyone else's lead is as unhealthy for believers as it is for lemmings.

We know from Scripture that in the last days many people will be running after this teaching or that teaching, and there will be little self-examination and even less Scriptural examination. These days our leaders too seldom encourage us to work through problems using the Bible as our guidebook. All the more reason to question where we are heading!

The New Testament church leaders, on the other hand, encouraged their followers to study issues through for themselves instead of just watching to see what other people did. Paul, you may recall, really thought a lot of the Bereans, when in Acts 17:11 he said, "Now these (the Bereans) were more noble-minded than those in Thessalonica, for they received the word with great eagerness, examining the Scriptures daily, to see whether these things were so." "These things" refers to what was being taught them, and we would do very well to follow their example today.

We trust the reader is examining all of the Bible passages quoted in this book to make sure that these things are so.

The fact that huge numbers of Christians now limit their family size proves nothing except that huge numbers of Christians are limiting their family size. This is an area of life in which our practices have not been scrupulously examined. It's time for us Christians to get back to the Bible, start accepting the blessing of children, and let the world follow us for a change.

Question 3
*Do you know how much it costs
to raise a child these days?*

All of us have heard that to raise a child from age minus nine months to twenty-one years costs several hundred thousand dollars. While those figures represent a typical American middle-class upbringing, though not necessarily a Biblical one, raising children *is* nonetheless a costly undertaking and your concern about money is a common question. This is readily apparent from the survey in Appendix B — "finances" was the most common response given when people were asked to list factors determining how many children a couple should have.

A question: Do we really believe that *we* provide for our children? We cannot in our own strength even provide for our own needs today. No father is the sole provider for his family, without God. That would be a most unbiblical position and that is why Jesus taught us to pray for the provision of our daily needs in Matthew 6:11, "Give us this day our daily bread."

We live our lives moment by moment, whether we make our livings recycling pop cans or as corporate executives for IBM. Those of us in the latter category might be tempted to think we have provided for our own futures, but stop and consider: one tornado, one earthquake, one heart attack, or one drunk driver on the other side of the road can wipe out all our finances. There is no bank vault so deep, no investment so secure, no health plan so all-encompassing that we can say, "OK, God, whether you send war or fire or flood or famine, I can take care of myself."

A newborn daughter is far less dependent on her parents for her sustenance than we are on God for ours. Why should we worry about feeding her, when God has promised to do the worrying about feeding us?

Attention, fathers, living a life of faith in God with regard to our family size may just be our Divine ticket to a better job. God declares that He is our real Boss, controlling jobs, promotions, bonuses, and the like. Asaph observed that, "For promotion cometh neither from the east, nor from the west, nor from the south. But God is the judge; He putteth down one, and setteth up another" (Psalm 75:6-7, KJV). Don't worry about how you will provide for your little ones. Your Father knows their needs better than you do. He knows it before you do (see Matthew 6:8) and He loves them more than you do. Just for reassurance, if the question of money is your real concern, race down to your Christian bookstore and get a biography of the life of George Mueller. If he could trust God for daily provision for the hundreds of orphans God had given him, we should not have any trouble trusting Him to provide plant food for our olive plots.

As Mueller gives us a great example of trust, so Hudson Taylor gives us great words of encouragement. He said,

"God's work done in God's way will not lack God's support."
The generating of children is no less God's work than the re-
generating of souls on the mission field.

Concern about the expense of children betrays a regretta-
bly short-term view, in any case. Writing in *World* magazine
(January 9, 1989, p.12), E. Calvin Beisner said:

> You know how the magazines love to tell you how much it
> costs to raise a child? Well, consider *these* statistics. The
> average person . . . will represent a combined liability, or
> economic cost, of $192,600 during his first 18 years plus his
> lifetime after retirement at age 65. But the same average
> person will occasion the production, directly and indirectly,
> of goods and services worth, if a male, $55,277 per year, or,
> if a female, $26,680 per year, every year from age 18 to 65.
> This means the average male occasions the production of
> $2,598,000 worth of goods and services during his lifetime
> and the average female will occasion the production of
> $1,253,960 worth of goods and services in her lifetime. This
> means the average male's net worth to society . . . will be
> $2,405,400, and the average female's will be $1,061,300 . . .
> figuring solely on the basis of measurable economic income,
> not including the tremendous value of the financially unpaid
> work people — especially women — perform at home.

Mr. Beisner got the figures from economist Marvin DeV-
ries, as reported by Allan C. Carlson in his book, *Family
Questions: Reflections on the American Social Crisis* (just in
case you wanted to know!).

Or to put it another way — the next time someone asks you,
"Why did you have all those kids?" you just answer, "to pay for
your Social Security." It never fails to stop them in their tracks!

The Puritan theologian, Adam Clarke, in commenting on
"Lo, children are a heritage of the Lord," from Psalm 127 in *A
Treasury of David*, wrote this:

To many God gives children in place of temporal good. To many others he gives houses, lands, and thousands of gold and silver, and with them the womb that beareth not; and these are their inheritance. The poor man has from God a number of children, without lands or money; these are his inheritance; and God shows himself their father, feeding and supporting them by a chain of miraculous providences. Where is the poor man who would give up his six children with the prospect of having more, for the thousands or millions of him who is the centre of his own existence, and has neither root nor branch but his forlorn, solitary self upon the face of the earth? Let the fruitful family, however poor, lay this to heart: "Children are an heritage of the Lord: and the fruit of the womb is his reward." And he who gave them will feed them; for it is a fact, and the maxim formed on it has never failed, "Whenever God sends mouths, he sends meat." "Murmur not," said an Arab to his friend, "because thy family is large; know that it is for their sakes that God feeds thee."

Reading in the same source as above we found that the Rev. Moses Brown had twelve children. On one remarking to him, "Sir, you have just as many children as Jacob," he replied, "Yes, and I have Jacob's God to provide for them."
So do we.

Question 4
Oh Rick and Jan, I go crazy with the kids I have now! You don't know what it would do to me to have . . . who knows how many more?

This question reminds me of a time several years ago when our number three child and first son, Adam, had just been born. It was a beautiful May afternoon and we had just brought him home from the hospital to our little 1 1/3 bedroom apartment. Jan, three year-old Staci, and two year-old Andi were napping, and as I looked at Adam's little form sleeping so peacefully in the crib I started to panic. Literally. Thoughts raced through my mind: "We don't have much money; I'll go crazy with another new baby." I remember my eyes filling with tears — not of joy but desperation. I understood just how a cornered animal must feel. So yes, I do understand your emotional reaction. I have felt the same way. What helped me withstand this emotional attack was realizing that God had caused Adam's new life and that He had given Adam to me for good and for a reward. Also, after Adam's birth we really started studying what the Scriptures said about having children.

For us, and others we have talked with who had many children, the toughest number to handle was two children. It seems to be that when the second little one pops onto the scene, many parents still have an infant or toddler. Thus, they are faced with two high-maintenance cases to handle. That can be trying! Plus, many parents (us included) think they are experts when they have only one child. But their second-born, very often more independent, may cause a radical drop in their self-confidence. By the third child, though, *Numero Uno* is usually a bit more self-sufficient and, if he or she has been properly trained, is actually beginning to be helpful. My big problem with Zachary, our eighth, is accessibility; I often have to ask one of the older brothers or sisters to let me hold him!

Scriptural discipline is a must in any family, large or small, or chaos will result and the joy that family life was meant to be turns into constant badgering, pleading, threatening, and anger. *What the Bible Says About Child Discipline,* written by Richard Fugate is unquestionably the finest book on child discipline we have read, perhaps because it is the result of 1600 hours of research into the Scriptures, not 1600 hours of credits in sociology, and therefore dispenses with the "you can appease your child into obedience" myth.

Jan is very fond of applying here what we mentioned in the previous question about the financial area. It is true that you cannot care for a dozen children. You in yourself cannot even care for *one* adequately. Our ability to bring up children in the way God desires is nil when done in our own strength. *But,* with His help, i.e., the counsel of His Word, our ability is multiplied. We might say that He who provides the progeny also supplies the ability.

There is another secret to this "I'd go crazy with eight kids" syndrome. We only get one child at a time! That is not too astounding to most people, but it was a true revelation to me. Jan and I didn't have eight children; we have had one child, and then one child, and then one child, and so on. Eight individual, perfectly spaced children. It all adds up to eight, and people who see us, see us in the present tense as a group of ten, but it took us sixteen years to gradually become so many. It's a big difference.

Another difference often forgotten is God's grace. When we had only Staci and Andi, God had not given us the grace to have the other six. I would have gone berserk! But His grace makes the Christian walk possible, and if God wants to give you a child, have no worry — He will also give you the grace to love and care for him.

Question 5a
*What will strangers think when they see us
with a large family?*

They will imagine that your I.Q. is somewhere between styro-
foam and yogurt.

Question 5b
What will my family and friends think?

If your family is at all sane, they will think you are crazy.
Ours certainly does! Just smile. As to what your church and
Christian friends will think, let me recount a humorous thing
that happened to us at our fellowship when we were still relatively new there.

As part of our Sunday School class on spiritual gifts, each
person wrote their name on a sheet of paper and passed it to
the next person. That person would look at the name, write
what spiritual gift they believed the person had on the bottom
of the sheet, folded their guess underneath so the next person
would not be influenced, and passed it on. Finally, each person got their own sheet back with a list of gifts, describing
essentially how their activities or interests were perceived by
the other adults of the church. When I got my sheet back I got
quite a shock! The great majority of listings said "Faith."

Faith? I could hardly believe it! Why in the world would so
many people, most of whom did not know me very well at all
yet, choose faith? I sat dumbfounded for about a minute, imagining George Mueller rolling in the heavenly aisles. And then it
hit me like a ton of kids — it was our (then) six children.

Allow God to bless you with children and you may be thought of as a modern-day Abraham due to your "great faith."

Question 6
If I have unlimited children, how will I ever have a career?

Take a deep breath and relax, because we are not going to have "unlimited children." We can only have God's limit of children. How comforting that we cannot over-reproduce!

Now ladies, about your "careers." First, as an opening exercise—a sort of warm-up—please consider trashing the women's magazines in your home. This purging may need to include a number of "Christian" women's magazines as well.

Next, let's get out our Bibles and open them to the letter Paul wrote to his co-laborer, Titus. We want the second chapter, verses 3-5. There we find a series of mini-directives from the apostle to different social groups within the local church.

When Paul gets to "older women," he details their ministry as primarily one of teaching. Who are they to teach or encourage? The *neos,* which means simply "young women." It will be very important to keep that in mind.

Now, what kind of lives are these older women supposed to encourage these younger women to have? Here, straight from Titus 2:3-5, are the seven characteristics of the younger women's career as God designed it:

- Love their husbands
- Love their children

- Be sensible
- Be pure
- Be workers at home
- Be kind
- Live in subjection to their own husbands.

The fact that Paul chose not to use the word for "mother" when speaking to young women about their life work, but instead through the Spirit selected *neos,* is very revealing. Among other things, it means that *all* young wives are supposed to be "pure," whether childless or blessed. They are likewise all supposed to be "sensible" regardless of their level of fruitfulness. And to remain hermeneutically consistent, each and every Christian wife is called to be an *oikourgos* — literally a "home worker" — no matter what she has been taught or has observed in her friends or church.

In Thayer's *Greek-English Lexicon of the New Testament,* the word *oikourgos* is explained: "Properly the (watch or) keeper of a house. b. Keeping at home and taking care of household affairs, domestic."

There is no question that Paul's readers understood what he meant. The word *oikourgos* was well-known, having been in use for at least five hundred years. *Oikourgos* is a straightforward and simple composite of two words and in its most literal sense is read, "the keeper of an inhabited house." *Voila* — a housekeeper!

Paul reinforces this concept in his directives for young widows in 1 Timothy 5:14, where he says through the Holy Spirit, "Therefore, I want widows to get married, bear children, keep house, and give the enemy no occasion for reproach."

The Greek for "keep house" is a different word than *oikourgos*. It is the word *oikodespoteo* meaning (better sit down, husbands), according to Thayer, "to be master (or head) of a house; to rule a household, manage family affairs."

Loosening your ties with clammy hands, men? Before you open the window and jump, the true picture to have (taken from Mary Pride's book, *All the Way Home*, 1989, pp. 170–172) is one of yourself as the CEO of your family, with your wife as the Plant Manager under you.

Now, building on this injunction that the wife is to be the manager of the home, we know that the Lord Jesus warned us that it is impossible to serve two masters (Matthew 6:24). The conclusion, ladies, is that your calling in life is to be a help-mate for the man God has given to you. Helping your husband is your life work and the prime focus of your earthly ministry.

The home is the Christian wife's domain. It is all yours! It is your "career," but more than just the world's myopic under-standing of what a career is — it is your center of ministry. Here are some examples of what you might be doing there: home business; evangelizing international students; hosting Good News Clubs; educating future Christian leaders (your children!); creating marvelous family memories; knocking down the crime rate (neighborhoods with alert women at home during the day get robbed *far* less often); interacting with politicians (the tele-phone and the mailbox bring them to you!); creating works of art; extending hospitality and encouragement to the lost and suf-fering; or preventing social problems by raising children who are not delinquents, drug addicts, unwed mothers, or welfare recipients. This is just *part* of the list!

Proverbs 31 depicts the life and wide-ranging activities of the godly homemaker. Smiling, Jan says, "There are not enough hours in the day . . ."

The working world tells you that its "fulfilling" opportunities like typing, filing, data entry, stuffing bottles in an assembly line, or soldering widgets in a factory are more satisfying than God's gift of actual lives to shape and mold and free time (with no time clock!) in which to do it. What a sad lie. The choice is black and white vs. technicolor holography.

God's way for Christian wives is unimaginably different than everything you hear from the world. He calls you to serve and be loved and protected by only one earthly master — your husband. Why surrender your freedom to try the impossible task of serving two masters at once? And why would a Christian employer do such a disservice to a sister in Christ?

One "given" in the opinion of many Christian writers of books for women today is the "necessity" of two paychecks in today's family. One wonders what necessities necessitate such a "necessity!" It is admirable to desire to sacrifice oneself to provide extras for the children, but for many, a list of "necessities" would include new cars (has the four-year-old learned to drive?), always-current fashions (does the baby care if he is wearing Reeboks?), vacations (most kids are quite happy to take in the sights in the old home town), new homes (where the parents get the twenty foot by sixteen foot master bedroom and the kids double up in a ten by ten), or savings accounts (in the parents' names).

None of these things are wrong, but God does not promise to give us any of them. Not one will make our lives fuller or richer. They may make life easier, but not necessarily better. None will cause us to become more like the Master or help build in us the fruit of the Spirit.

Our family, like many others, has lived without the above things for years, and we are certainly no worse off than if we had any or all of them. Again, we certainly do not begrudge those who have much of this world's goods, but we can say that a family of ten can live, be happy and, yes, even content, on twenty thousand dollars a year.

The point of this is not to lock anyone in the stocks of guilt. But, if a wife or mother has left her true life calling — for things or for "personal growth," we would lovingly urge her to reassess her priorities. Or, if as is increasingly common, the husband is prodding his wife to get out and earn some money, he had definitely better do some serious study on what it means to be the head of his family "as Christ is the head of the church." The "Mr. Mom" idea is cute, and the practice is burgeoning in our churches, but the concept is Scripturally indefensible. Tilling the ground was Adam's work, not Eve's. God's design for the roles of husband and wife is crystal clear. God will always supply needs through the husband. If for some legitimate reason (college being far from one!) the husband cannot supply basic food and clothing, then the church, not the keeper at home, must. That is the Biblical blueprint.

How does all this tie in with the question of birth control? Well, unless a woman is in the habit of flying to work wearing a red cape and a large red *S* emblazoned on her blouse, she will not likely be able to do her duty to both a large family and an outside-the-home job. Employers are very aware of this, which is why back in the sixties women applying for a job were frequently asked as a part of the official job interview if they were using birth control and even when their last period was!

The boss in the working world wants *all* of you. If a woman wants to truly succeed working for another person in the business world, she can expect to work long, long hours and have little control of her schedule. Today, middle managers average 50 hours a week and top executives are putting in an *average* of 65 hours a week! Even union workers, who traditionally at least benefited from a rigid limit on the hours they had to work, are having to deal with mandatory overtime work. With this kind of lifestyle, a woman just can't do much more for her children than simply produce them and pick their custodians. If she lets pregnancy and maternity leave slow her down too often, she can forget about advancement altogether.

Not that aggressively pushing for advancement is exactly the ideal. God's twin character goals for women are found in 1 Peter 3:4: "But let it be the hidden person of the heart, with the imperishable quality of a gentle and quiet spirit, which is precious in the sight of God."

We have observed that a job outside the home makes the development of these two precious qualities enormously difficult.

Jan and I faced this choice years ago when, at a conference, we were challenged in our hearts to let Jan stay home and be a homemaker. The hard part was that I was in graduate school and everybody knows that when a husband is in school the wife has to work. It's the American way! But we prayed, Jan quit, and very soon God gave me a job on campus with flexibility for my schooling and just enough money to live on. As Jesus said in Matthew 6:33, "But seek first His kingdom and His righteousness; and all these things will be added to you."

Question 7
You go to the doctor when you have an illness, don't you? Why not use medical expertise in this area? What's the difference?

A good question. We have certainly been asked this before. It was troublesome for some time, until we studied the Word of God on this whole "fertile" subject.

Hopefully, chapter three answered this question, but for those still wondering, maybe it will help to identify the real problem behind the question—the person asking it still thinks having kids is bad and God thinks it is good.

We go to the dentist when our tooth hurts so he can fix a negative situation. Pain and disease, though completely under God's authority and in His plan, may be accurately considered negative situations. The Savior healed ill and diseased people. He raised Lazarus from the dead. He calls His own out of darkness into the light of eternal life. He fixed and still fixes negative situations. But having children is a *positive* condition, not a negative one! God Himself says so (Psalm 127).

You may have seen the bumper sticker that says, "If it works, *Don't fix it!*" Amen! That is why this question is a bit crazy. It would make more sense to visit your auto mechanic with your new Mercedes and say, "Fred, this thing runs too well; it's too fast and it gets way too many miles per gallon. Couldn't you botch it up a bit—maybe pinch the fuel line or switch a couple of the plug wires?" There is no need to ask medical science to fix something that God has working just the way He designed it to.

God has given man dominion over the earth, but never have we been authorized to usurp His plans in our own bodies, His temple. The Christian must give Him dominion to control his or her own body. Our bodies are meant to be a living sacrifice, as per Paul's urgings in Romans 12:1: "I urge you therefore, brethren, by the mercies of God, to present your bodies a living and holy sacrifice, acceptable to God, which is your spiritual service of worship."

Question 8
Aren't we supposed to use common sense in this area of living?

To be blunt, what is meant here by "common sense" is worldly reasoning, blind to faith and wisdom. Again, some of the earlier chapters have shown that true Biblical wisdom calls for us to trust God.

Coming in out of the rain is one thing. Denying God's control in an area He has the complete right, ability, and desire to oversee is quite another.

Godly wisdom, as differentiated from common sense, *always* directs us to selflessness and a life characterized by being as malleable as the potter's clay. Trusting God is being *truly* sensible!

I memorized a verse as a very young Christian which years later has taken on new meaning,

> Trust in the LORD with all your heart,
> And do not lean on your own understanding.
> In all your ways acknowledge Him,
> And He will make your paths straight.
> (Proverbs 3:5-6)

Could it be that "all your ways" includes reproduction?

Question 9
What about the rhythm method?

The rhythm method (which in its most sophisticated form is now called Natural Family Planning) was developed as an alternative to "artificial" methods of birth control, such as pills, condoms, diaphragms, plastic explosives, etc. As far as it involves simply becoming aware of your biological cycles, it is neutral. It is thought to be useful both in the avoidance of pregnancy and in the attainment of it. The actual results, of course, are controlled by God.

We do find it ironic that in an era in which many are teaching and talking about how the physical portion of marriage can be more enjoyable, especially for wives, Christians advocating the rhythm method teach women to avoid sex during the time of the month when God designed the female psyche to be most responsive to it.

In actual practice, Christians using natural family planning often start out using it as birth control and then, as they loosen up, start having more children on purpose. We guess this might be because NFP both costs more than "normal" birth control (in terms of a more straitjacketed physical relationship) and because it makes the connection between sex and reproduction much clearer than any other form of contraception. Couples using NFP as birth control are not actually likely to conceive any more often than couples using any other system, but they are perhaps more vividly aware of God's ability to overrule their efforts, and more inclined to turn around and eventually start cooperating with Him. The real truth about NFP, though, is that it still may be an accurate gauge of the heart. We are not too thrilled about trusting God to accomplish what is best for us—we still feel that He needs our help. When a couple realizes God's true part in conception, along with other truths for the Word, they realize that NFP is simple needless tinkering with a system He already controls lock, stock, and baby.

Question 10a
My doctor told me not to have any more children.
Shouldn't I do what he says?

The white-coated words, "I'm sorry, but you had better not have any more children due to possible health risks," may be greeted with inner joy — almost bliss! No more 2 A.M. wake-up calls; no more diapers; no more bottles; no more maternal measurements of planetary proportions; *no more blessings!* We may cover up our glee with a sober face and intone something like, "Oh, that's too bad . . ."

Medical questions can be some of the most difficult to deal with in a book like this, due to the fact that each case is so different. Fortunately, there are some helpful general principles to remember.

Should a medical person tell you "no more children," ask yourself, "Do I inwardly crave children as tokens of God's rewards toward my spouse and me?" If you do desire children, please do not stop with the opinion of one doctor. Get several opinions and let those people know that you *want* children. You might say, "Doctor, my spouse and I would really like to have another child. Isn't there some way?"

The average doctor understands that a great many women want no more children. If he hears the opposite from you, he may try harder to work with you, after he gets some medical attention himself — for shock!

We are assuming that your doctor is truly unbiased about pregnancy. This might not be the case. One reason to be extremely skeptical of doctors bearing tidings of great "unjoy" is that OB-GYNs have been educated to encourage you to have few children. Following are some quotes taken from books used in the training of today's doctors:

Purvis L. Martin, M.D., in *Handbook of Office Gynecology* (Grace and Stratton, Inc., 1985) says on page 39,

> Overpopulation is an increasing threat to the world today. China, a nation with the world's largest population (no more than 1 billion), appears to have achieved close to zero population growth. But India and large emerging nations of Africa and Latin America face continually rising rates of human reproduction. The United States appears to have reached zero population growth in the most affluent sections of the population, although not among the underprivileged. There still exists a large need for medical assistance in family planning in this nation. *Leadership in meeting this need falls partly to the gynecologist, largely in office or practice.* (Emphasis added)

Here are two adorable little quotes from *Gynecology and Obstetrics: The Health Care of Women* (McGraw-Hill, 1975), pages 2 and 33:

> Rapid growth of population has become second only to nuclear warfare as civilization's greatest menace. *The gynecologist-obstetrician has assumed a leadership role and has recognized the necessity of controlling human fertility . . . (by) birth control, abortion, and sterilization . . .*

> Lowering fertility rates involves . . . couples acting almost invariably in opposition to not only the teaching of their churches, but also to the laws of their countries, and the moral standards of their societies . . . *people must come to want fewer children.* (Emphases added)

The above quotes show current gynecological training ideas. The next two show the direction gynecology is heading.

Professor Eugene B. Brody wrote an article in 1983 entitled "The Context of Desire. Reproductive Choice in an Era of Coercion and Freedom." It was published in *The Young Woman (Excerpta Medica,* 1983). Here's a tidbit:

> Aldous Huxley, as early as 1933, predicted the development of ovum factories for the production of workers, and in vitro fertilization and artificial insemination are already available to women who want and can afford them. These still require the woman to nurture within her own body a growing organism involving a male element. My prediction for the future is that rather than dispensing with the male and making her dream for self-sufficiency come true, women will dispense altogether with the wish to have a baby as we now know it, and baby production will not only take place independent of sex, but will be separated from her body as it is now from that of the male.

Huxley would have loved this harbinger of Big Brother Baby Banning. Says *Jeffcoate's Principles of Gynecology,* 5th Edition, revised, Tindall, Butterworth's, 1987, page 599,

> *Improvement of Stock*: As the human race increases, there is much to be said for limiting reproduction to those individuals showing the best physical and mental attributes. This, however, implies interference with the rights and happiness of the individual and, *at present,* is wholly contrary to medical ethics. (Emphasis added)

I'm sure glad we live "at present!" That is how our OB-GYNs are being trained!

God presents various authorities to us in His Word. Medical professionals, for all their training, are not our authorities. You should feel free to question, even scrutinize, their motives and outlook and to express clearly your own ideas, no matter how strange those ideas may seem to them.

The doctor is working for you as your skilled professional employee. You are not under his rule.

It would be helpful and wise to let him know your convictions. If you find a doctor who ridicules you or tries to persuade you to change your convictions, even if the doctor is a believer, find another. You might do even better to find a midwife, since midwives are trained to support the family through pregnancy and childbirth rather than to cut Fallopian tubes or scoop out wombs.

We can offer three suggestions in the search for an OB who will be supportive:

- He must be pro-life. In this qualification you can be assured that the doctor has a correct appraisal of the value of human life.

- It will be great if the physician has a large family himself. He may be more sympathetic to your desires.

- Though we would not make this an absolute criterion, how good it would be if he patterned his practice after the Great Physician.

Question 10b
What if my doctor has told me that I'm too old
to safely have any more children?

For years the number "35" has been like a "NO TRESPASS-ING" sign in the bearing of children — okay before thirty-five, *verboten* after. What follows is a lengthy quote which appeared in the San Jose *Mercury News* in 1984. It gives blessed help to would-be Moms who have been held captive by an otherwise perfectly good number,

You've often heard that pregnant women over 35 are at greater risk. Statistics, you've been told, show that prematurity, longer labors, Caesarean sections and genetic disorders including Down's syndrome are more common among after-35 first-time mothers than among those 34 and under.

But this is not exactly the case.

"The idea of the high-risk pregnancy for women over 35 is a myth, and probably was all along," says Phyllis Kernoff Mansfield, Ph.D., assistant professor of nursing at Pennsylvania State College. Her thesis, *Advanced Maternal Age and Pregnancy Outcome: A Critical Appraisal of the Scientific Literature,* should send shock waves through the medical establishment.

Mansfield maintains that there has been no consistent scientific evidence to suggest that age 35 is some kind of turning point in a woman's childbearing life. If there is a problem here at all, she says, it's with the quality of research as well as the expectations of many obstetricians.

Obstetricians have had difficulty accepting delayed motherhood, Mansfield points out. In typical medical jargon, the mature mother-to-be is referred to as an "elderly primagravida." A 1958 council of obstetricians defined this term arbitrarily as any woman over age 35 expecting her first child. It immediately identified her as a high-risk patient.

"In the years that followed, doctors sought statistics to confirm their hunches," Mansfield discloses. "They found what they were looking for in hospital clinics. There, just as they had predicted, the 'elderly' were plagued with such pregnancy complications as premature labor, low birth weight and genetic disorders. The trouble is," she adds, "many women studied were not representative of the general population and typically had far more health risks than one would expect in a well-controlled study."

"To conclude from this data that all women over 35 are at high risk—or that age alone is a risk factor during pregnancy—is totally irresponsible," Mansfield states. "There was never a clear-cut, high-risk age factor for healthy, educated women."

Unfortunately, well-designed, properly controlled medical studies on actual risks for postponed pregnancies are scant. In one of the few significant studies, doctors monitored pregnancy, labor and delivery of women at the crest of their childbearing years—45 and over. During a 17-year period, 23 such women passed through the delivery-room doors. All had normal, healthy babies, and only one was born premature. There were no still-births, no congenital abnormalities, no Down's syndrome. Although typically the rate of Caesarean-section deliveries is high for such women, 19 delivered vaginally. Only two women had prolonged labor. In fact, four went through labor in less than three hours (*Journal of Reproductive Medicine,* May, 1971).

In a more recent study, comparing a much larger group of older pregnant women to younger pregnant women, the conclusion was the same. "Delaying pregnancy, said the researchers, "does not constitute a particularly different problem and is not dangerous to the women either during pregnancy or at the time of delivery" (*Obstetrics and Gynecology,* August, 1980).

Physicians' attitudes play a big part, too. In fact it's been suggested that the trepidation that often goes along with a thirty-five-plus pregnancy is largely the fault of the ill-at-ease doctor.

The high rate of Caesarean sections for women 35 and older is a prime example. One researcher wrote, "Perhaps because science and technology have made Caesarean section a relatively safe procedure, the obstetrician thinks of this maneuver first in managing patients he has been mentally conditioned to accept as high-risk individuals."

The truth of the matter is in contrast to what many women are led to believe: Older women are even *more* capable of going through uncomplicated vaginal deliveries than younger women. That was illustrated in a study conducted on 50 healthy middle-class professional women 35 years of age and older around Washington, D.C. For 33 percent of the women, it was their first pregnancy.

Fully 50 percent went through labor and delivery completely unmedicated, a significantly larger figure than for younger mothers. A total of 89 percent delivered vaginally, better than the 72 to 75 percent range for all mothers regardless of age. And only 11 percent delivered by Caesarean section, which is much lower than the 25 to 28 percent of all mothers. All had healthy, normal babies (*Papers in the Social Sciences*, 1982).

Older women tend to do better psychologically, too. "Rather than fear or feel intimidated by the physical aspects of labor and delivery, older mothers are consistently described by physicians and themselves as more relaxed, more in tune with themselves and appreciating rather than resisting the physiologically trying process," reports the researcher, Iris Kern, Ph.D., a professor in the department of social welfare at the University of the District of Columbia.

There you are, older Moms-to-be. Not only is it safe to let God bless you, but you may do better in your pregnancy and delivery than much younger mothers. You're not getting older, you're getting better!

Question 10c
No, I'm serious. I have major health problems
which will kill me if I have another child.

Surely the most loving thing a husband could do for a wife
who *really* was at death's door physically would be to leave
her alone sexually and give her body a chance to recover. God
says one aspect of genuine love is it "does not seek its own"
(1 Corinthians 13:5). In other words, a Christian man, convinced of a fatal pregnancy, would sublimate his sexual desires to his wife's good and display true, self-sacrificial love.
Sex under such circumstances, assuming that a serious health
problem *really* exists, would be simple untamed lust and not
"doing unto others as ye would have them do unto ye."

If you're too sick to have babies, you're too sick to have
sex.

On the other hand, the husband may well suspect that the
wife's horrible medical problems are overblown, either by her
or by her doctor (see Question #10a). Doctors, for all their
training and desire to provide good health care, are often
wrong. And let's not forget that God has a way of miraculously healing people, too—sometimes through the very pregnancies that were supposed to kill them.

A recent issue of *A.L.L. Issues* featured a poignant story
that illustrates how God can use pregnancy in surprising ways.
The doctor-author of the story had a married female patient in
the very last stages of dying from tuberculosis. The problem
was that she had a gaping hole in her lung, and the doctors
just couldn't get it to stay closed long enough to heal. The
woman requested permission to be home with her family at

Christmas, if she survived that long, and the doctor granted it, thinking she would never make it. After returning to the hospital, she continued to hang on to life by a thread. Then, six weeks later, the woman began to lose her ability to keep her food down. Tests showed that God had given her a fantastic Christmas present — she was pregnant. The doctors naturally thought of abortion — such a sick woman couldn't survive the stress of pregnancy, and she was going to die before the baby could possibly be born anyway. The mother absolutely refused to have an abortion. Then the miracle happened! She started to gain weight. And as the baby grew larger, *her womb began to press against the hole in her lung, sealing it shut.* The hole healed; she had the baby; she went home.

We all saw the media hoopla over the husband who fought for and gained the right to order an abortion for his comatose wife. Doctors had advised him that carrying a baby to term would kill her. What the newspapers probably didn't tell you was that in the one known case of a comatose woman giving birth, the woman *began to recover* immediately afterward. This is just as we would expect, since as Jan would testify, it's hard to sleep while giving birth!

We would not discount all medical testimony about the hazards of pregnancy for women with serious physical conditions. But serious physical conditions have a way of discouraging sexual activity, or even (in some cases) making it physically impossible. If God has put it into your heart to desire your husband sexually, and into his heart to desire you, could He perhaps have put it into His plan to care for the result?

Question 11

*Didn't God have Psalms 127 and 128 written
for an agricultural people? Many children would
definitely be a boon in a farming situation.
Most of us don't live that way today, though.*

Somehow, somewhere, sometime, somebody got the idea that kids are good for one thing—farming. While ours do love playing in the dirt, is their "blessingness" restricted to the manual labor we can get out of them?

We must realize that the writer of Psalm 127, King Solomon, was about as far from being a farmer as you can get. He did not say, "Like plows in the hand of a farmer, so are the children of one's youth; how blessed is the man whose silo is full of them."

No friends, God has an incredible vision and plan for your family. It is exciting, wonderful, individual, *and* you can find it in the final chapter.

Question 12

How can I spend quality time with a dozen kids?

That is a very good question. Not to put it off, but in chapter nine Jan will speak to that issue. History helps us, too. Remember Susanna Wesley.

Question 13
God has led us to have "X" kids. So there!

In our survey (Appendix B), one of the most mystifying things was the number of people who answered the question, "Are you sterilized?" with a "Yes," and the question, "What factors should a couple use to determine how many children to have" with "The Lord will decide" (?).

Doesn't it seem queer that God would say one thing in His Word and turn around and tell us something else?

Let us ask, how does God lead His children? He leads through His "living and active" communication with us — the Bible (Hebrews 4:12). The Holy Spirit uses the Word to give direction to the child of God.

The idea of God whispering to you the exact number of children you should have first of all introduces revelation above and beyond the Word, and secondly, can be a work of Satan.

Strange doctrines are afoot these days, and this subjective wandering away from the authority of the Scriptures is one of the most dangerous.

God's Word includes all you and I need to know about our ultimate family size; He knows what it should be and can make it happen.

"God has led us," may simply be a smoke screen thrown up to cover the truth that we just plain don't want any more kids. In fact, few American men would dare ask their wives the question Elkanah asked Hannah, "Am I not better to you than ten sons?"(1 Samuel 1:8). The answer we'd expect today would be, "Big deal! *Anything* would be better than ten sons!"

Question 14
Doesn't this no-birth-control philosophy mean
we only have sex in order to have babies?

Actually, only one person has said this to us. I assume he was referring to the panic caused by the thought of "unprotected" intercourse. Naturally, neither you nor we believe that sex is *only* for fertilizing eggs. God is far more creative than that!

Two things need reinforcement: First, pregnancy is *not* going to occur except through God's active agency, and second, God obviously had reproduction as well as pleasure in mind when He designed our bodies. His initial command to Adam and Eve was not "Have a blast, guys!" but "Be fruitful and multiply" (Genesis 1:22).

What is there to worry about? Nothing! Given the very real possibility of conception using any birth control method, there is always a "chance" of conceiving, which should keep any birth control practitioner uneasy who knows his contraceptive statistics. So we discover quite a paradox here. Rather than birth control practitioners being at ease, actually it is only those who feel no need to force their control in these matters who can relax and enjoy a truly worry-free relationship.

Question 15
If we use birth control, isn't God free to overrule
and give us children whenever He wants, anyway?

Of course. He is easily that powerful. But we are straining to see if the tip of the mast is polished on a schooner with a five-foot hole in the keel. We may recall that Satan attempted to cause the Savior to throw Himself off the pinnacle of the temple using just such logic.

The problem is that our attitude is still not aligned with God's. He may want to give us gifts. We do not want to receive them.

Yes, He may overrule us. But here is another possibility — a distressing one. Psalm 106:14b-15 says, "And [the Israelites] tempted God in the desert. So He gave them their request, but sent a wasting disease among them."

That "wasting disease" was the plague of Numbers 11:33. The King James version translates the phrase as "leanness to their souls." He may sovereignly allow the measures we take to ensure no more children, but see to it that it is not well with our souls.

Once in a Sunday school class on finances a friend agreed with the teacher that Christians should remain debt-free. But he then defended the use of bank cards as necessary in order to establish a line of credit, so he could go deeper into debt! The question we are now answering is fraught with just such problems. We want to throw roadblocks in God's way so He can overrule us? We want to aim for barrenness so God can give us conception? Is it not more likely that, like the father of a stubborn child, He will give us just what we want but we will end up not liking it when we get it?

If God can do something "difficult" like bypassing contraceptive roadblocks, is it not logical that He can do something "easy" like simply not giving conception? If He is going to *take* control, why not submissively *give* Him control? Why get Him angry at you?

Question 16
Why bring children into such an evil world?

First of all, you are dead right about this being an evil world. In scanning the American scene, not to mention Australia or Great Britain or France or Russia, we are faced with a scene of increasing decadence. One wonders if ancient Corinth or Rome had anything on us. Those poor civilizations were disadvantaged, not having the blessing of our small convenience stores with their pornography, our sensual addiction to rock music, or the cancer of godless television programming which has destroyed the morality and desensitized the heart of the nation. This does seem like a bad place to bring a guest.

Going back to square one, *we* bring no one into the world (we know you know). Now, to retool our thinking a bit, let's stand up and recite: "The children God gives us we will train to be leaders in this desperately sick world." There is an oath to make the Hippocratic ill by comparison. Our children will, if God blesses, grow up to be the answer to many of the world's problems. After all, in just fifty years almost none of us reading these pages will be here. The world always belongs to the next generation.

On the other hand, the children we *don't* have can't be a blessing. And it's only since the church endorsed family planning — and thereby cut down its size over the next fifty years to about one tenth of what it could have been — that the world started sliding downhill so rapidly. Hmm . . .

Imagine if medical schools shared the outlook of the above questioner. "There are too many diseases — we quit!" Our kids are not victims. They are the solution!

The Israelites spent forty extra years in the wilderness because they were too worried about their children being taken into captivity by the Canaanites to get busy conquering them (see Numbers 14:3, 23). Instead, the Lord told them in verses 31 and 32, "Your children, however, whom you said would become prey — I will bring them in, and they shall know the land which you have rejected. But as for you — your corpses shall fall in this wilderness."

Is there a lesson here for us?

Question 17
*Doesn't this position lend itself
to a particular theology?*

While doing some work in the home of a very nice Catholic mother a few years ago, she inquired as to the number of children I had. We had six then and she quipped, "You must be a very religious Protestant or a very dumb Catholic!" She expected that if any Protestant was willing to have a large family, he must be more than ordinarily devoted to God — which is fine by me, as we *all* ought to be more than ordinarily devoted to God!

The truth of God's Word should always be discernible to any true child of God. Ultimately, as a friend said to me, this whole book boils down to one's view of the sovereignty of God. If our view of God is that He is really our Lord, none of the rest of this book is necessary. If He is not Lord of all, can He be Lord at all?

Question 18
I believe all this, but the thought of letting go petrifies me! What can I do?

That may well be *the* question for most of us. Whenever you or I become frightened or anxious in any situation, it is most often because we are focusing on the wrong object. Remember Peter's aquatic stroll? As long as he kept his eyes on the Lord, all was fine. But, when he looked down, away from Christ, he got wet feet—and then wet everything. It would be surprising if there aren't some who have made the decision to give God total reproductive control who never get just the slightest bit edgy. Keep looking to Jesus and quote Psalms 127 and 128. It will pass. As you realize you are being guided by the omnipotent, infallible Master, your fear will turn into joy. Quiet is the climate in the center of His will.

Question 19
What is so bad about using something as safe as the birth control methods we have today?

Aside from the fact that the preceding five chapters (and those to follow) point out that children are a blessing and it's not our job to rid ourselves of blessings, there are no "safe" birth control methods.

The morning this was being written found me neck-deep in books on contraception at a university medical school library. What I found on the various contraceptive methods was very sobering, especially since the writers were all proponents of these methods. Did you know the morning-after pill is made out of coal tar? Might as well have a chilled glass of STP for a wake-up drink in the morning.

Below is a listing, compiled from a number of books, on troubles with the various types of man-originated birth control.

Condoms: clumsy, not totally reliable, with possible manufacturing flaws and possible allergic reactions in husband and wife.

Diaphragms: possible allergic reactions, urinary tract infections, pelvic pain, cramps, urinary retention, bladder symptoms, foul-smelling or profuse vaginal discharge (any foreign body in the vagina can cause this), messy, often destroys any spontaneity to lovemaking.

Contraceptive foams, creams and jellies: some contain toxins which may or may not be absorbed through tissues into the system (much debate on this), possible cause of allergic reactions, messy.

Intrauterine Devices (IUDs): Here are the blessings the experts tell us can occur when using an IUD (listed in order of frequency): spotting, bleeding, hemorrhaging, anemia, cramping, pain, partial or complete expulsion of the IUD, lost IUD strings, infections related to the strings, difficult removal, uterine perforation, embedding, cervical perforation, and pelvic inflammation.

The real tragedy and horror of the IUD use is explained below in an article from the June 1986 *Omaha Christian Action Council Commentator.*

The *primary* mechanism of the Intrauterine Devices (IUD's) is *abortifacient* (abortion inducing). While they may occasionally prevent conception (i.e. fertilization; that is, where the egg and the sperm unite in the fallopian tube), this is not the main mechanism of action. When conception occurs, the fertilized egg (a new human being by every medical and Biblical definition) arrives in the uterus 6 to 10 days later. If an IUD is in place, this tiny human encounters a hostile uterine environment and is unable to implant itself into the uterine wall. Thus, he or she is *aborted*—the IUD has caused the death of this new life in the uterus.

This is why the Food and Drug Administration now label the IUD's as "anti-implantational," describing them as working at the uterine level (6 to 10 days post conception).

Sophisticated studies of women wearing IUD's have shown that frequently they demonstrate positive pregnancy tests (Beta HCG serum levels) that then become negative again over a period of time. This, of course, demonstrates that conception has taken place and is then followed by the death of the young person.

These sobering facts have led most Christian doctors (and informed Christian couples) to reject the IUD as morally unacceptable. *They are* not *contraceptives!*

Those are the main types of birth control. Three have been left out. One is sterilization, which gets a chapter of its own (the next one). The second type is a very natural type of birth control which God Himself designed and the third is the *pill*. The second type is used more than any other "method" in the world. It is lactation or breast feeding.

Space does not permit a study of the various levels of hormonal activity during the nursing period, but we think you would find it an interesting area of study. How fascinating to discover God's workings in these areas and to see just part of His plans as they operate in the wonder of the female body. The best book on this subject is *Breast Feeding and Natural Child Spacing* by Sheila Kippley (Cincinnati, OH: Couple to Couple League, 1989). For additional information about this subject, contact the La Leche organization in your area. They have facts and figures which are very helpful.

The third method, which deserves its own heading, is *the pill*. There are many who believe that the birth control pill has had more to do with changing the sexual climate of our half of the world than any other single source. That may be true. If so, then it is an overwhelming curse, physiologically, socially, and spiritually.

We have another quote, from the *Omaha Christian Action Council Commentator*, concerning the distressing mechanism by which the "pill" can work.

> The "birth control pill" is also not mere contraception. Although it is designed primarily as a contraceptive, it is not always effective as such . . . and when it is not effective, it has a "back-up" mechanism that is clearly *abortifacient!*
>
> The "pill" has three mechanisms of action. You may easily look them up in the Physician's Desk Reference.
>
> 1. It attempts to suppress ovulation. When successful in this action, an egg is not released and conception, of course, cannot occur.
>
> 2. It thickens the woman's cervical mucous. Thus the sperm are restricted from moving up the reproductive tract. This is also contraceptive.
>
> 3. However, the "pill" *causes* certain changes in the uterine lining so that if conception does occur, the new life meets a hostile environment when it arrives in the uterus 6 to 10 days later. It cannot implant. It dies. This is abortifacient.
>
> Why, then do some Christians continue to accept the "pill" as a morally acceptable choice in planning families? One attempted justification centers upon the uncertainty of just how often the "pill" works as an abortifacient. Unlike the IUD, such persons might argue, the "pill" is primarily contraceptive by suppressing ovulation most of the time. (The

most obvious exceptions here are the "mini-pills" which
have no estrogen and allow ovulation to take place 40-60
percent of the time. This is published in Emory University's
Contraceptive Technology.)

Initial studies showed the early "pill" formulations (which
were much more likely to suppress ovulation due to their
higher doses of estrogen) still allowed "breakthrough ovulation" to occur 1-3 percent of the time. However, one scientist at the National Institute of Health (NIH) publicly stated
that the lower estrogen dose "pills" of today allow ovulation
up to *50 percent of the time!* Dr. Thomas Hilgers, the renowned fertility expert who is currently the Director of the
Pope Paul the Sixth Research Institute, was present when
this statement was made though the NIH has never published this information. In fact, the NIH has been more than
a little hesitant to publish specific data in the medical jour-
nals to which private MD's have access. The drug compa-
nies are similarly reticent to provide such data. Neverthe-
less, the scientist mentioned above was at that time the head
of the pregnancy research development branch of the NIH,
itself the spearhead for contemporary medical research.

So, then, how often does the "pill" have to rely on this abor-
tive "back-up" mechanism? No one can tell you with cer-
tainty. Perhaps it is as seldom as 1-2 percent of the time . . .
but perhaps as frequently as 50 percent of the time. . . .

Does it matter? The bottom line is that it is impossible for
any woman on the "pill" in any given month, to know
which mechanism is in effect. In other words, the "pill" *always* carries with it the potential to act as an abortifacient!
Therefore, can Christian couples truly neglect the awesome
ramifications that use of either the IUD or the various "birth
control pills" create? Those Christians who are sincerely
committed to God and His Word must also strictly obey His
clear mandate "Thou shalt not kill." This is a most impor-

tant message which Christian couples must hear and heed. (Emphasis added)

That is the story on how safe contraceptives are. As to the effectiveness of the various methods, here are the standard figures (see table 5:1). The figures indicate the approximate number of pregnancies per 100 woman-years. That term refers to "the number of women who would become pregnant in a year while using the method correctly and consistently."

Table 5:1
Method of Contraception and
Number of Pregnancies

Method	Pregnancies
Rhythm (non-NFP type)	13
Condom	3-5
Diaphragm (with spermicide)	2-3
NFP	2
Intrauterine Device	1-2
Oral Contraceptive	0.5
Vasectomy	0.15
Tubal Ligation	0.04
Lactation (as described in Sheila Kippley's book)	0 (the first year) — Average time to first fertile period is 12.4 months using total breastfeeding, which includes night nursing, no pacifiers, and no solid foods until six months.

Based on the previous information about methods of preventing a new life from being given to your family, especially the *pill,* why anyone would seek to wreak havoc on their wondrous reproductive systems with artificial birth control methods is a total mystery — especially when natural mothering provides *natural* child spacing. Well, maybe it's not a total mystery. In such a decision we may again be displaying the attitudes of our first parents in their desire to become gods.

Here is a new rendition of a very familiar song. It will not hit the top of the charts, but it may hit the nail on the head. It is entitled "At The Pharm(acy)" and can be sung to the melody of the hymn, "At the Cross":

> At the Pharm,
> At the Pharm,
> Where I first bought the Pill,
> And the burden of my heart rolled away;
> Now it's me in charge,
> No, my family won't be large,
> But in everything else have Thine own way.

Question 20
Doesn't the Bible talk about birth control at all?

We are so glad you finally asked! Yes it does. There are three passages to study. The most well-known is 1 Corinthians 7:5. It says, "Stop depriving one another, except by agreement for a time that you may devote yourselves to prayer, and come together again lest Satan tempt you because of your lack of self-control."

Unfortunately, this passage hardly supports a pro-birth control position. In it we discover, among other things, that the rhythm method is unacceptable. Paul is teaching that there is a time not to have normal relations. However, that time is not allowed so that we can attempt to stymie God's workings, but for times of extended spiritual exercise. The focus is on intensifying your spiritual life, not on preventing babies.

That was not much help for the birth control camp. Neither is the next passage, Leviticus 12:1-5, which states:

> Then the LORD spoke to Moses, saying, "Speak to the sons of Israel, saying, 'When a woman gives birth and bears a male child, then she shall be unclean for seven days, as in the days of her menstruation she shall be unclean. And on the eighth day the flesh of his foreskin shall be circumcised. Then she shall remain in the blood of her purification for thirty-three days; she shall not touch any consecrated thing, nor enter the sanctuary, until the days of her purification are completed. But if she bears a female child, then she shall be unclean for two weeks, as in her menstruation; and she shall remain in the blood of her purification for sixty-six days.' "

In other words, when a woman had a boy, she and her husband were to abstain for forty days. When she had a girl the period of time doubled to eighty days. If the directions are followed, a couple will obviously not have children every nine months.

Medical science is now aware that there are hormonal differences in the mother depending upon whether a boy or girl has been born. That could possibly be God's reason for the differing periods of abstention. But regardless, it is clear that while a wife who has just given birth is still bleeding, even today we would be wise to abstain. (Most women are more than willing to follow this advice!)

Finally, Leviticus 15:19 states, "When a woman has a discharge, if her discharge in her body is blood, she shall continue in her menstrual impurity for seven days; and whoever touches her shall be unclean until evening."

The principle of abstaining during the monthly flow is coupled, in Ezekiel 18, with not committing idolatry or adultery, not oppressing or committing robbery, feeding the hungry and clothing the naked, not being a loan shark, judging fairly in disputes, and following God's decrees. This principle, then, would seem to stand today, even if the "seven days" part of it is ceremonial. This fits well with what medical science tells us about the increased chances of infection and disease caused by intercourse during menstruation. It's always interesting when medical science discovers the *why* behind what God has said!

Some Christians abstain from sex just during the time of flow. A small group observe the seven-day abstention period. An even smaller group, including many orthodox Jews, interpret the time of monthly abstention to last fourteen days. Surprisingly, we have numerous testimonies from the last group that this abstinence *improves* their marriages, including their sex lives. In any case, it is clear that Biblical abstinence related to the period does *not* occur during the fertile time. Rather, the husband is saving up a "charge" which is likely to make him *more* fertile when the time of abstinence is over!

➤   ➤   ➤

There were the twenty questions. We hope we anticipated and helped answer whatever questions you may have had. The next chapter deals with a mushrooming practice in the church — sterilization.

Focus

- How does Biblical revelation (chapters one and two) interface with the questions we have?

- How does the exercise of faith affect our question?

- It may be advantageous to have defenses prepared for others with questions.

- What is there to fear in entrusting God to superintend our families?

7

STERILIZATION AND REVERSALS

W e finally found out what causes babies and we've fixed it." So joked a friend not long ago. He went on to explain that he had just had a vasectomy. He and his wife had had several children within the span of a few years and were afraid of having any more.

That was one of the times I would have given much to think faster. Much faster. In fact, I would have liked to answer his comment before he was even in the position to make it.

Who Is Doing It?

Every hour of every day, men and women who belong to Jesus Christ decide to surgically end their ability to have children.

The Statistical Abstract of the United States (1987 edition) reports the following facts about the numbers of women who have been sterilized:

- One in four women between the ages of fifteen and forty-four is sterilized, or her husband or partner is.

- The breakdown is:
  One in thirty-eight between fifteen and twenty-four years old,
  one in four between twenty-five and thirty-five,
  three in five between thirty-five and forty-four.

- Nearly two out of every three married women are unable to have more children.

In early drafts of this book, this section on sterilization was much shorter, consisting of only a few paragraphs in the sixth chapter. When we started tabulating our surveys of Christian attitudes towards the blessing of a full quiver (the results are in Appendix B), it became apparent that a much fuller treatment was warranted. The survey results give no reason to believe that the sterilization statistics given above would be very different if applied to the church.

Sterilized Christians

Should the statistics be different for Christians? Or should Christians be equally as anxious as the world to diminish our numbers and impact? We seem to be doing just that. We also seem to be confused on the issue, as there was a major split among those who participated in the survey as to whether sterilization was allowable at all; 69 percent allowing for sterilization and 31 percent forbidding it, some in very forceful language.

We have many good friends who have chosen this path. Some of them have had reversals (1988 medical statistics indicate that approximately 1 percent of those who become sterilized will later seek a reversal). Others want to retrace their steps, to undo the damage, but find that they lack the several thousand dollars required. Our family prays almost daily for a Christian couple who made the decision to have a vasectomy years ago, before becoming Christians. They now deeply regret it and greatly desire more children than the two joys they have. The needed funds simply are not there yet and we grieve with them and ask God to provide the money for the reversal.

Likewise, we know of several believers who have had vasectomies and tubal ligations reversed. One couple we know made a two thousand mile trip to have a vasectomy reversed. They are praying fervently for a child. Another couple has had a tubal repaired and God blessed them with a baby. The joy of the conception God later gave was to them a true miracle; one they had feared might never happen.

We know couples who have read this book or with whom we've discussed these issues and they have no arguments or questions. They simply will not trust God. They may opt to be moderately fruitful and add instead of multiply. They choose to fill perhaps one or two bedrooms of their home rather than the world. We just try to encourage and pray for them, remembering that once that was exactly *our* state. If the couples have a deep desire to be godly and to follow Christ in their marriage, God will make the necessary changes in their lives.

In the meantime, should you be one of those couples hovering on the edge of this decision, or who are already sterilized but had never realized a reversal might be possible in your case, here is some food for thought to help you add another arrow to your arsenal!

Eight Common Reasons for Sterilization
(and Why They're Wrong)

Cathy Hier from California wrote an eloquent letter, published in the first issue of Bill and Mary Pride's newsletter, *HELP*, that sums up the major arguments for sterilization—and then demolishes them—better than we can. As a mother of five who got sterilized, then obtained a reversal, and since has been blessed with another baby, here is her story:

> Don't do it! I wish I could tell the whole world—*don't do it.* Don't voluntarily let yourself be robbed of the ability to give the gift of life. I am thoroughly convinced that besides our own life and breath, the most precious thing God has given us is the gift of giving new life (babies).
>
> Well, what happened was exactly how you are feeling: baby-after-baby, what about giving more of ourselves to the older kids, always tired and worn out, husband working nights for only half the needed money, demands, demands, demands. . . . Well, by the time Jane was about seven months old, we felt the same way I think you do. We talked it over, prayed about it, and came up with a few basic answers.
>
> If we stop having more kids we can:
>
> 1. Give more to those we already have.
>
> 2. Not struggle so much financially.
>
> 3. Not be so tired.
>
> 4. Mom could get back into shape, energetic instead of worn out.
>
> 5. Mike's parents would be relieved.

6. I wouldn't feel like I was burdening the nursery and Sunday school with all my kids (terrible commentary on the state of the church).

7. We could get back to a normal routine without constantly upsetting the household with a new baby every year.

(Now #8 is the major one we convinced ourselves with, and look how silly it seems now.)

8. More babies truly would be a blessing (the Word of God is true), so we will be denying ourselves a blessing—BUT the Lord knows our weakness, and He will forgive us.

Can you believe that is the attitude we went into the vasectomy with?

I bet I know what you're saying. You're probably saying, "It doesn't sound so strange to me. . . ."

Well, when you still have little crawlers hanging on your knees, and little yukky diapers to change, there is *no way* you can imagine the emptiness *of being without* a new little one. It was shallow of us to say, "We know we'll be refusing a blessing, but God will forgive us." Because *until we couldn't have* another baby and *our last baby wasn't a baby,* all of a sudden we *really regretted* the vasectomy.

Oh yes, before I continue the history, I left out a reason we rationalized the vasectomy. . . . I was pressured to "go to this," "teach at that," "be a leader," "have a ministry." . . . Finally I said this is *not* right, I'm *staying home* for my family. . . .

At first (after we decided to have no more children) it was exciting to sew new clothes that weren't maternity, and to exercise to flatten my stomach, and get compliments for being in shape after five kids. And it was thrilling to be able to be finished with laundry and housework for a change—to have a breather once in a while, to have the work I did last for a while. But now I'm ready to trade all that for more babies.

And you know what? *The kids* want more babies. They aren't any more content with an energetic non-pregnant Mom than they were before. I think we transfer our selfishness to them (and also nourish their own selfishness) instead of just trying to mature in the Lord and become givers instead of takers.

We never told anyone about the vasectomy but now we feel we owe it to people to share our mistake. . . . Now I can't even count the number of people who regret their irreversible decision. It's too bad that it's so easy to get it done.

Health and Safety

Concerns about health are another major reason couples choose to be sterilized. Sterilization is promoted as a completely safe alternative to "dangerous" pregnancy. As we have already seen, the definition of when pregnancy is "dangerous" is extremely cloudy, depending often more on the doctor's preconceptions than on any scientifically verifiable facts. Now we will also see that sterilization is not quite as safe as we all have been taught.

Sterilization is strange. In other surgical procedures, defective organs or systems are repaired or replaced. The emphasis is positive—to cure an ill. But in sterilization we happily go under the knife to ruin a system which is functioning just as God intended.

Vasectomy Risks

The male reproductive system produces fifty thousand sperm every minute. God has designed ways for their release naturally, especially in the one flesh relationship of marriage. But after vasectomy, the little wigglers can't get out. Where do they go? Into the man's body, where his immune system must now tackle the formidable task of destroying his own seed.

Is this harmful? Well, we can find clinical studies supporting any position we like, and it seems that every few months another study is announced, crying "Safe" or "Unsafe." Whom are we to believe? We suggest bypassing the studies, which can't study the long-term effects because those results won't be in for another forty years. Consider God instead. He certainly didn't design the male reproductive system to cannibalize sperm continuously over a long period of time. He considers children a gift. And just as other perverse sexual practices are starting to leave a wake of disease, we wouldn't be at all surprised to discover all sorts of unexpected ill effects from this attempt to thwart God's design for the male body.

In this age when AIDS and other diseases stemming from a weakened or destroyed immune system are ravaging millions worldwide, I, for one, wouldn't pay a nickel for an operation that insulted my body's immune system in this way.

Medical Consequences of Female Sterilization

And what about the risks of female sterilization? Alida Gookin from Mississippi said in the same issue of *HELP,*

> I don't think your book [Mary Pride's *The Way Home*] mentioned all the medical risks involved in sterilization. Over 40 percent of women with tubal ligations have gynecological problems (excessive bleeding, etc.). About half of these be-

come so serious as to lead to the need for hysterectomy. This changes hormonal balance, especially in the case that ovaries are also removed. One friend of mine, after this operation, went through menopause though she was only in her thirties. Result: Dried, wrinkled skin like that of an old lady. Metabolism change, resulting in weight gain, the "matronly look. . . ."

While citing several medical studies in both Britain and the U.S., the Couple to Couple League's pamphlet on *Sexual Sterilization* said, "The figure of a 40 percent increase in menstrual problems as the result of tubal ligation seems standard." (One study said 43 percent.) Furthermore, a study cited in the *American Journal of Obstetrics and Gynecology* found that the rate of cervical cancer experienced within three and one-half years after tubal ligation was 250 percent (3 times) higher than the normal rate. In a study cited in the *British Medical Journal,* 18.7 percent returned for a hysterectomy. This figure represents almost one-half of those who had continuing problems following the surgery.

Some women who have had a tubal ligation had "menstrual disturbances requiring hormone treatments. . . ."

Planned Parenthood statistics that were published in the Memphis *Commercial Appeal* said that 25 percent of forty-year-old women have had a hysterectomy. Based upon the information I have cited, plus the testimonies of several women I know who have had hysterectomies, I wrote a letter to the editor asking why Planned Parenthood, in its zeal to further popularize sterilization, did not mention that hysterectomy may be a side effect of female sterilization. Several days later I visited my gynecologist, and the registered nurse with many years of experience there said she saw my letter in the paper and agreed that I was "absolutely right. . . ."

If Planned Parenthood is correct in reporting that a fourth of all forty-year-old women have hysterectomies, shouldn't we ask why? If any other human organ in middle-aged adults came to be diseased and required surgical attention as much as the womb does, there would be a demand to know what is causing such problems.

Sexual Sterilization can be ordered from the Couple to Couple League, 3621 Glenmore Ave., PO Box 111184, Cincinnati, OH 45211-1184, if you include twenty cents and a self-addressed, stamped envelope. This little pamphlet has some fascinating facts about the medical consequences of sterilization that you definitely ought to read before going under the knife.

Why Hasn't Anyone Told Me This Before?

You are probably surprised to hear about the health risks associated with tubal ligation, since the doctors who perform this lucrative operation have made a point of promoting it as safe and virtually risk-free. The woman who develops hormonal problems or other symptoms after her tubal may not make the connection, and if she does, she is likely to be told her case is unusual. Bollixing up the entire female reproductive system is supposed to be a perfectly normal procedure without any side effects. Supposedly God designed women to have slit Fallopian tubes and (in the case of hysterectomies) missing uteri!

Jean M. van der Linden from Victoria, Australia wrote in the third issue of *HELP,* "You may be interested in this newspaper clipping which appeared in our local paper about two years ago, which supports the theory that tubal ligation does have an aftermath. That is not surprising. Interfere with the finely tuned instrument our bodies are for the *wrong reason*

and there is a price to be paid. God's approval does not rest
on these operations."

The article read as follows:

> Last year about fifty thousand Australian women had an op-
> eration called tubal ligation (sterilization) to prevent them
> from having children.
>
> Now a Melbourne doctor says he is disturbed by complica-
> tions such as heavy bleeding and the rate of hysterectomies
> after sterilization.
>
> In a research paper in the leading British medical journal,
> *The Lancet,* Dr. John Cattanach, of Hawthorne, said the
> long-term complications of physical and psychological
> trauma are caused by damage to a small artery during the
> operation.
>
> Dr. Cattanach's theory, based on his research when practic-
> ing at Lilydale, is that damage to the small artery, which
> runs close to the fallopian tubes of the uterus, restricts blood
> supply and estrogen production.
>
> This finding seems the key to the whole sad mystery of suf-
> fering after the tubal ligation. Adequate estrogens are essen-
> tial to the physical and psycho-sexual well-being of women.

A Sterilization Story

Statistics are, of course, bloodless beasties. Countless sterilized sufferers have stories to tell about their supposedly "risk-
free" tubals that make our point more poignantly than any
number of statistics about X percent of sterilized women who
suffer from bleeding, pain, drastic mood shifts, and other
"minor" inconveniences.

Dee Smith from Arizona shared this story in the third issue
of *HELP*:

I underwent a tubal ligation in June, 1981. Because my husband and I were divorced and I was sure I did not want to bring any more children into this world (or so I thought), I saw no other recourse. However, in June of 1984 the Lord began to deal with me. He showed me that what I did in essence was to have an abortion because I cut off the life which could have begun. . . . As I shared with a friend (who also had a tubal ligation) what I knew she seemed surprised and at the same time relieved to hear what was said. You see, the Lord had shown her the very same thing!

We began to see that our bodies are not our own as we are bought with a price, and we are to glorify God in our bodies (I Cor 6:19-20). We are to present our bodies as living sacrifices (Rom 12:1, 2).

Over the last few years, I have run into many other women who in trying to walk in a pleasing manner before God have also seen the same things in regard to sterilization. Most of these women have had other developments in their bodies which can be traced back to their tubal ligations. One major development is a sense of mourning and the lack of understanding as to why it's there. The mourning is for the babies who aren't in their lives. Hormonal balance is definitely affected!! I can attest to that myself.

Read in Deut. 28 about the blessings and curses and you will see that barrenness is a curse — even a self-imposed barrenness. Look at Exodus 23:26, Deuteronomy 28:4, 11, 15, 18, Leviticus 26:9, 22, Deuteronomy 7:13, 14. Children are a blessing from God, not a curse. God said we would not be barren if we walk according to His design. . . .

I paid for my disobedience (even though I was not yet living my life for Him) four days after the tubal ligation. I was readmitted into the hospital with severe stomach pain — so severe you could not touch me without the pain being unbearable! I underwent exploratory surgery. They found a puncture (the size of the end of a large straw) in my lower bowel caused *during* the tubal procedure! Caused *by the cauterizing machine spark* during the tubal!

I have since repented and God has been faithful. My heart says if He wishes for my husband and me to have more children we know He is the healer! We have since remarried and know that God is sufficient.

If I have learned anything through this, it is that God is faithful. He has seen me through this and I can warn others. TRUST GOD to determine how many children you are to have and enjoy each one fully!

Reversals

Medical technology offers us the opportunity, through God's blessing, to rectify an action which may have been made in a moment of panic, not prayer. We would encourage our sterilized brethren very strongly to seek a reversal and then pray for God's blessing.

Some wonder if God will heal them so they don't have to save up for an operation. There appear to have been miraculous healings of sterilizations, but try to save up money. And let your requests be made known to God—and your church. God has designed the church to meet many of the needs of its fellowship. Financially blessed believers ought to actively seek out those who want a reversal but cannot afford it—and pay for it—and pray for it! If you do not know anyone, please write to us, and we will send you the names of Christians who want more children more than anything in the world, and who would be *eternally* grateful. No mutual fund or money market could offer such a return on your money.

Medical statistics tell us that about one percent of those who are sterilized will seek reversals. Of that number, only 20 percent will be successful (this number varies widely from doctor to doctor). However, a friend of ours has been in touch with dozens of Christian families who have sought reversals, and her experience has been that the success rate among these families is close to 100 percent. We think that the discrepancy in these figures might well reflect God's blessing on His people who at last become committed to seeking the blessing of children.

Nothing is sweeter than seeing a picture of one of these miracle babies. May Heaven rejoice that extra plates need to be put on for the Marriage Supper of the Lamb, because more little ones are being invited to the dinner!

Many of the most important events in Scripture involve God giving babies to barren women: Sarah, Rebekah, Rachel, Hannah, and Elizabeth. Truly, "He makes the barren woman abide in the house as a joyful mother of children" (Psalm 113:9). As the Psalm goes on to say, "Praise the Lord!"

If we have sinned either willfully or in ignorance by discounting God's blessing of children, let us do our best to redeem the situation, and let God do the rest. Then we can have quiet consciences and (God willing) noisy little feet pounding about the house!

Focus

- Consider the implications of the following three statements: Sterilization is not the crucified life. Sterilization is not a Spirit-led decision. Sterilization is self.

- For support from other families who have experienced sterilization and reversals, and up-to-date information on this and other subjects, you might consider subscribing to HELP. For information write to Home Life, P.O. Box 1250, Fenton, MO 63026.

- What do you think of the statement on page 131 equating sterilization and abortion? What are similarities and differences?

8

A WORD TO SINGLES

I n the next chapters we will be looking at what it means to a father and mother to trust God to bless us with children. But first, what about single readers?

Most of this book has been written with married couples in mind. But surely some who are not yet married are reading it as well.

An unmarried soul may feel, "Hmmm, . . . if *that's* the way marriage is supposed to operate, do I really want to get married?" Don't panic! If on the morning of my wedding you had told me that one day Jan and I would have eight kids, she might still be waiting for me at the altar. Or if you had asked me then how I liked children, the answer would have been "From a distance." But you know what? It's really not bad at all. In fact, I actually *love* having a large family!

The Special Ministry of Singleness

If you feel that God has a ministry for you which would require you to be gone much from your home, you may want to

seriously consider singleness. It really cannot be too bad, for
Paul makes these singular remarks in 1 Corinthians 7:7-8,
"Yet I wish that all men were even as I myself am. However,
each man has his own gift from God, one in this manner, and
another in that. But I say to the unmarried and to widows that
it is good for them if they remain even as I."

Permanently-single people have an opportunity to drive
single-mindedly towards evangelistic and spiritual goals.
Those blessed with this gift are not weirdoes with no sex
drive, but rather Christians with an *additional* ability to handle
life without the help of a spouse. These are the people who
should be Christ's front line soldiers on the mission fields and
in other hazardous assignments. Married couples, on the other
hand, are good for the mopping-up and long-term necessities
of discipling the nations, since they can model so many Christian relationships in their families. As Liane Jablonski of Massachusetts noted recently in *HELP* issue number five:

> It is quite common for missionary couples to delay having
> children in order for them to concentrate on a specific situa-
> tion that requires complete time involvement and/or to send
> the children they do have away to school for social *and* for
> work/time reasons as well. They often say that the only cir-
> cumstance under which they would do this is for the Lord's
> work, which takes precedence over their own normal desires
> for family. It occurred to me that Paul addressed that sub-
> ject, but his answer was not to not have children, but NOT
> TO BE MARRIED. In 1 Corinthians 7, Paul indicates that
> he believes being single is really the best way to concentrate
> on God's work, while allowing that being married is not
> wrong and is appropriate for some people. Since in the same
> chapter Paul definitely speaks against any length of celibacy
> within marriage (the only truly reliable form of birth con-
> trol!) maybe singleness should be the (so to speak) form that

birth control should take for those who are truly in time-pressure situations, such as Bible translating/teaching for remote tribes when they are literally the only people (outside of the unsaved tribal people) who know the language and are Christians, and the guerrillas are moving in fast?

Preparing for Marriage

Let's assume that you have not been granted the gift of celibacy. How, then, should you prepare for marriage, with its special responsibilities and blessings?

Looking backwards, we married couples could offer some counsel. Start building your future home's spiritual foundation now. Strive to build Christian discipline and habits before marriage.

Another thing, especially applicable to men — finish your education and training, and as much as God allows, get established in your law firm, assembly line, or home business. Then get hitched to your sweetie.

Does that seem like an off-the-wall line of counsel? Is Solomon off-the-wall? Proverbs 24:27 offers this solid, if generally ignored advice: "[Put first things first.] Prepare your work outside, and get it ready for yourself in the field, and afterward build your house and establish a home" (Amplified Bible).

A single woman might contemplate avoiding marriage because of her health. If you *know* that you are not healthy enough to have children, you may want to consider being married only to Christ. In Corrie Ten Boom's book *The Hiding Place,* she remarks about her sister Betsie, "Betsie had always known that because of her health, she could not have children, and for that reason had decided long ago never to marry." If you will not be able to bear children, any prospective husband should know that. Such knowledge could be God's way of directing you to stay single, as it was for Betsie.

If you simply do not want to have children intruding into your life, please plan to remain single. That is a far better choice than getting married and still trying to live like a single. On the other hand, if you are now planning to be married, please get together now and agree on what you're going to do about family planning. It may be the single most important area for the committed Christian man and woman to agree on before joining their lives together. It is also much easier to come to an agreement *before* marriage than after.

In the survey we conducted, you will see that over 98 percent of the singles who responded said that they would not choose to allow God to control their reproduction. The reasons were varied, but the sentiment was unified — birth control would be their choice. Even when they admitted that a large family (defined in the survey as more than three children) had more advantages than a small one, they shunned the idea of having one themselves.

But just maybe the Scriptures have opened your eyes to the truth that God indeed has the tools and a kind enough disposition toward His children to do what is best for us in our child-bearing.

What does this mean to single Christians?

Several things. For starters, when dreaming of a happily-wedded life, let your daydreams put a few children into the scene (they are very inexpensive to imagine). When we set our hearts on cars, travel, careers, and ministries and later realize that children do take up a chunk of time and income, experience shows that we tend to choose the material over the eternal.

The church has always fought against materialism, but now the challenger is a super heavyweight. The world can throw at us a dazzling array of electronics, sports, clubs, and a sufficient number of hobbies to occupy a hundred lifetimes. New Testament writers were generous in their counsels to "Set your mind on the things above, not on the things that are on earth" (Colossians 3:2). While that is tough today, Paul in the next verse states why we can do it: "For you have died and your life is hidden with Christ in God."

Many of us who have been married awhile would like to have the early years of our marriage back to see if God might have added another token of His blessing to our marriage. We have empty spaces around our tables that God may have filled for us.

The single Christian planning to marry has the opportunity to sail a straight course from the altar. God is a Captain who will only give you what is best for you and your future spouse. For the soon-to-be-married man, our prayer for you is the greatest marital blessing found in all the Word of God: "May the LORD make the woman who is coming into your home like Rachel and Leah, both of whom built the house of Israel" (Ruth 4:11).

Now, with this perspective in mind, let's dive into the chapter on how to handle fatherhood in a BIG way!

Focus

- What things might be included in the Proverbs 24:27 concept for a single man?

- What benefits might accrue to a couple who followed this counsel before entering into marriage?

- Why do couples so tenaciously seek to block such a blessed event?

9

A WORD TO HUSBANDS

B y this point, you might wonder how this doctrine of divine planned parenthood works in real life. This chapter is basically a place to record some thoughts, observations, and practical insights that were not presented before — some "down home uncommon sense" especially addressed to fathers and fathers-to-be, straight from a father-that's-been eight times already!

Here is the proposition: A child of God need not use birth control. You don't need it. When people say to me, "You are anti-birth control!" (and therefore anti-intelligence and un-American), I say, "No, I believe wholeheartedly in birth control. But the Scriptures prove that God Himself is our birth Controller. He controls the conception, spacing, and birth of the children He gives so completely and so perfectly that I have absolutely no reason to take over the responsibility." That is no "pat" answer, as it has taken God several years to teach me that. It is theologically sound, unimpeachable truth. If we come to God and give Him our future family size and spacing, do we really imagine He will turn it down, ignore, or punish us?

Having said that, let me announce for all to hear why you may still feel that you must control your family size.

You're Scared!

"Hey, Rick, you didn't have to say *that!*" Sorry, but for some it is the truth, and we shouldn't be ashamed to admit it.

I'll start True Confessions by admitting that for a long while I was intimidated by this whole concept. Yet God is very aware, after watching quite a few of us for quite a few years, that as finite folk we become frightened when we have to follow a course with no idea of where it will end up. And that is certainly the case here, is it not?

While reading this book, you may have had visions of walking down the aisle of your local grocery store surrounded by legions of grubby, runny-nosed little tykes. Well first, it's always a good idea to carry a handkerchief. Then go ahead and admit you are queasy — it will help you feel better. But still, you can guess what will happen — your acquaintances will discuss you sometimes, wondering if you are losing touch with reality.

To encourage yourself, spend time reading biographies of God's great men and women. You will be impressed by how "out of touch with reality" they were perceived as being by their families and even by other Christians. Jesus was not understood; His disciples were not understood; so it follows that these greats of God were not understood. So why should you be? But consider this — you have a unique opportunity, if God should so bless, to be a leader for Christians around you.

Here is another thought. God may elect to give you *no* children if you give Him the choice. The National Center for Disease Control informs us that one American couple in four is unable to have children. If you find that after a reasonable period God is choosing not to give you children, that may be a direct signal that He has some sort of a ministry for you which will require unusual flexibility and/or availability.

But for the majority of us that will not be the case. We will have children. Some may have quite a few. God will provide for them all, you can be sure, and the blessing of seeing Him provide will be a joy to your life and a powerful heritage to pass on to the grandkids.

Now, what are the nitty-gritties of having a large family?

Money

In one section of our city the price of new homes starts at hundreds of thousands of dollars. I realize it is possible that God may want us to have one of them some day, but I can assure you, if that is true, that is His vision and not ours.

I do know from the Bible that God will care and provide for us. The Lord Jesus said in Matthew 6:31-32:

> Do not be anxious then, saying, "What shall we eat?" or "What shall we drink?" or "With what shall we clothe ourselves?" For all these things the Gentiles eagerly seek; for your heavenly Father knows that you need all these things. But seek first His kingdom and His righteousness, and all these things shall be added to you.

"All these things" includes providing a place to live. God knows what we need. He has a dwelling place for us in heaven and will also take care of our housing down here.

Many of us will not have fortunes to spend on things. Don't worry about keeping up with the Joneses. Your children are far more valuable than the Joneses' four VCRs, spa memberships, or summer homes in Vermont. So what if much of our income is invested in our families? Christians live forever, you know, which is more than can be said for gym equipment, fishing rods, and 4x4s. What we spend on those things is gone when they are. What we spend on our kids can bear fruit until Jesus returns and also provide us with treasure in heaven. Find me a better way to "take it with you!"

Guys, you may consider selling your 300ZXs, Miatas, Vettes, and all those other cutesy Fisher-Price Car of the Year finalists. Getting a van or station wagon will save you money on insurance.

Fine dinners at Italian restaurants with Roman arches may be replaced by eating more often at the Golden Arches or standing on your fallen arches barbecuing hamburgers on your own backyard grill. Do you get the picture? If the picture bothers you, you can ask God to make you totally content with simple things (the real secret of the happy life).

Alternatively, the needs of a large family might drive you to develop your own business and you might end up far richer than you would have been otherwise. (For information and resources on how to start your own business, see Mary Pride's book *All the Way Home.*) Economic researcher George Gilder found that having a large family caused men's income to *rise* (see *Men and Marriage,* [Gretna, LA: Pelican Publishing House, 1986]).

Whether it is due to God's direct blessing or to extra dedication to work on the part of family men, the fact is that you simply can't predict poverty for the parents of large families. You *can* predict that believers with large families will be taken care of. As King David, the father of a large family, said in Psalm 37:25-26:

> I have been young and now I am old;
> Yet I have not seen the righteous forsaken,
> Or his descendants begging bread.
> All day long he is gracious and lends;
> And his descendants are a blessing.

Time

If you actually give God *carte blanche* in your reproduction, it is very possible that He will actually shower you with blessings. What will that change about how you spend your time?

Well, the city-wide mania here is softball. Omaha is known as the softball capital of the world because it has more teams per capita than any other city. I know men who actively play for two or three teams per week, plus substitute when needed on other teams and play in tournaments on many weekends. Commitment to softball often equals four or five nights a week.

Not to be a spoilsport, but we just cannot do something like that to our schedule and lead a large family to follow Christ; or a small family; or even a small wife. The addition of children will mean the subtraction of other pursuits; maybe important pursuits, maybe just trivial pursuits.

The issue is not quality versus quantity time. Jan and I are grieved when we hear people say that they don't have much time to give to their kids, but what time they do have is "quality" time. We know there are days when almost all parents have time to do with their kids is say "Hi" because of an unusually busy schedule; that's not what we are referring to.

Our goal, so much as we can accomplish it, must be to aim for *quantities* of quality time.

We have found that quality time cannot be scheduled. It sneaks up on us, and if we are too busy to seize it, sometimes we lose priceless opportunities to frame a life situation with a Biblical truth.

Most readers have heard messages on Deuteronomy 6:6-7, but here it is again for a refresher, "And these words, which I am commanding you today, shall be on your heart; and you shall teach them diligently to your sons and shall talk of them when you sit in your house and when you walk by the way and when you lie down and when you rise up."

God intends for us to spend as much time as possible with our blessings. Now, how do we do this?

In agricultural settings, a son could assist his father in his chosen field, but it is often not practical or possible to take your six-year-old to work with you at Merrill Lynch or the construction site. It is therefore imperative that we spend as much time as possible outside of work with our children — going to the store, getting gas for the van, or running errands.

I was challenged as I read that Jonathan Edwards had the habit of taking one of his eleven children with him when he went places, even on preaching trips. That so inspired me that it is now my goal, whenever possible, to take one of our children with me as I go somewhere. Jan often does this as well. The rotation is youngest (no newborns!) up to oldest and the kids love it. Sometimes the trip is for a 75-foot walk to the corner store to get a gallon of milk. Other times it is two hours of errand-running. We've had some very good times, one-on-one.

Our time is not our own. The more children we're given, the truer it is. But we have an excellent example in the Lord

Jesus, who spent His available time with His twelve spiritual children. We men must abandon our tendency to leave parenting to our wives and follow the example of the Lord Jesus. We are the trainers of our children.

Worried if you will be able to stand the sacrifice of giving up your time? As one who has been there, let me reassure you that you will be rewarded many times over for giving more and more of yourself to your children. Strange as it sounds, going for a walk with a little person and communicating with him on his own level what God has been teaching you can be more satisfying than Monday night football, or Tuesday night bowling, or Wednesday night softball.

Every man has the chance to be a king to his kids. Or he can opt for being a face in the crowd in the world and a stranger at home. Guess which is more satisfying!

The Numbers Game

You mathematicians may have looked down the road and said to yourself, "A child every two years; I'm twenty-six now; menopause at fifty-one, that's twenty-five years; *That's twelve and a half more kids! Aarghhhhh!!*"

Now, now, settle down. God may have no more children for you — or eighteen — or five — or nine — or one. Even if every couple you know had twelve kids (and you know they don't), God could still choose a different number for you. You aren't a statistic; you are an individual, and God has a unique plan for *your* life.

Check out these Bible statistics, all from families that not only eschewed family planning but actively desired children.

- Abraham and Sarah — One boy
- Isaac and Rebekah — Twins
- Jacob and Rachel — Two boys
- Jacob and Leah — Six boys and one girl
- Jacob and Bilhah — Two boys
- Jacob and Zilpah — Two boys
- Joseph and Asenath — Two boys

The other sons of Jacob had between one and ten sons, with most averaging between three and five. These figures hold true for most of the families of the Bible. The only absolutely enormous families were those where the man had more than one wife, which I trust is not the case with you!

The Joys of Fruitful Fatherhood

Here are a few advantages of being given a large family:

- The satisfaction of living under God's direction
- The joy of seeing many come to the Savior
- The excitement of experiencing God's provision
- The blessing of having a household in which a number of spiritual gifts are operating
- The opportunity to learn sharing
- Always having somebody to play with (the kids like this, too!)
- Filling up your own pew in church

- Learning to delegate and divide responsibilities

- Being a positive example of faith to other Christians

- Developing a profitable home industry

- Having many helpers in your quest to learn patience

- Never having to suffer in silence

- Fielding your own NBA, Major League, or NFL team. We can now have a five-on-five male vs. female basketball game. While the two youngest boys are not great shooters, you should see how they dribble!

- Leading your own string quartet, brass quintet, glee club, choral society or symphony orchestra

- Tax deductions galore

- Excellent traction in snow

- Satisfying your collector's instinct

- The kids finally wearing out their Carter's baby clothes

- Practicing Deuteronomy 6:6-7 and 2 Timothy 2:2 disciple-making in the comfort of your own home

- You have never lived until you have been "ground-zero" in a family free-for-all in your living room like we often have in ours!

One group has not yet been addressed to the degree they deserve to be in this book. That group is faithful Christian women. It is fine for us men to sit and theorize about this and that, but you ladies are the ones most physically affected by the decision to trust God with your family size. Therefore, I now turn the typewriter over to the woman without whom Staci, Andromeda, Adam, Stefani, Daniel, Alexis, Micah, and Zachary (and we have just learned one week before this goes to press–Arrow number nine!) would not have been possible: my very favorite person and excellent helpmate, Jan.

Focus

• What should the Biblical reaction be to seeing a large Christian family?

• What are some concerns or fears a man may experience as he contemplates the potential of receiving many bouncing baby blessings?

• Personalize Deuteronomy 6:6-7 by replacing *"you"* with your name and *"your sons"* with your children's names. Then write it out, frame it and hang it where you can see it often.

• Let's face it, numerous pregnancies, childbirths, newborns, and older children can be physically wearing on a woman's body and emotions. What specific steps can husbands take to make things smoother for their wives?

• Men, how well do you know your wife? Can you predict what your wife's deepest feelings are in the area of God-controlled fertility?

10

A WORD TO WIVES

T hank you, Rick! I appreciate the opportunity to share the
woman's point of view.

Several years ago we had a refrigerator repairman in our
home. Adam, six years old at the time, asked him if he had
any children. When he admitted that he had two, with a third
on the way, Adam shared the exciting news with me. I asked
the ages of our repairman's children and discovered that he
and his wife would soon have three under two and one-half
years! I made a comment like, "Wow! That's really exciting!"
His reply was, "I think so, too, but my wife isn't so sure. She
wishes they were a little farther apart."

Would that be your response, too? It's fine for a *man* to be
writing about family size. He doesn't have to go through a
summer pregnancy, when it is so hot that breathing is a chore,
let alone cooking or housework. Or a winter pregnancy, when
you can't find a coat to fit and your family thinks you are
crazy for letting your hot feet hang out of bed even on the
coldest nights. Or not being able to see your shoes, let alone

tie them! Or heartburn and varicose veins! And then there is always labor and delivery!

Up the Organization

Women who ask me, "Are these *all yours?*" generally respond to the information that, yes, they are, by saying, "You must be very patient and organized." In other words, they think only patient and organized women ought to consider having "many" (e.g., more than two) children.

Is it true that normal childbearing is reserved only for saintly types? Are only patient and organized females the prime candidates for motherhood? I'm glad I didn't think so before I applied for the job! Although I am learning both qualities, I was not born with them. That may have been one of God's reasons to add many children to my life in the first place. As Paul put it, "Not that I have already obtained it, or have already become perfect, but I press on in order that I may lay hold of that for which also I was laid hold of by Christ Jesus" (Philippians 3:12).

How do we learn patience? James 1:3 says, "The testing of your faith produces endurance." It's the trials that bring patience.

When we ask God for patience, He does not give us a heart full of endurance and say, "Now go your way!" He brings special testings and opportunities, designed especially for us as individuals to produce the proper degree of endurance needed for our lives.

One of my favorite stories on the subject is from Volume 2 of *Streams in the Desert*:

A young man went to an aged saint on one occasion and asked him to pray for him, saying, "I find myself giving way to impatience continually. Will you please pray for me that I may be more patient?" The old man agreed. They knelt together and the man of God began to pray: "Lord, send this young man tribulation in the morning, send this young man tribulation in the afternoon . . ." The young man nudged him and said, "No, no, not tribulation, *patience!*" "But," said the old saint, "it is tribulation that worketh patience! If you would know patience you must have the tribulation."

I may have more opportunities to *practice* patience than some other mothers. I may also *look* organized! I can do six things at once, as mothers are expected to do. But I too get frustrated by the things that do not get done. My kitchen floor, for instance. It went months without being well-scrubbed until a dear friend came to help me out during my recovery from gall bladder surgery.

Just like you, I am learning how to get organized as I go along.

God does not usually give four or five children to us all at once and say, "*Get organized!*" Most of us start out with one and go from there. And then, when you have a supportive husband and many smaller hands added, you end up with quite an organization!

Home Free

God made us to be creative beings, and has provided us mothers with the perfect environment to use that creativity. What a challenge and what an honor! However, according to the outside world, and maybe even some Christian friends, we cannot truly be fulfilled unless we have an "outside ministry." They may agree that we should be at home, but add that we must be active somewhere else as well. They fear that if we are not, we will be in danger of not giving the proper appearance of Christianity to the world, or we will be missing out on something, or God will be displeased!

Here is where we need to begin rebuilding our thoughts and lives on God's principles. The world's ideals have so subtly crept into the church that it is hard to determine the truth from the lie! Titus 2:3-5 states very plainly God's plan for women whom He chooses to be wives. Rick already referred to Titus 2:3-5 in chapter six (question #6), but here it is written out:

> Older women likewise are to be reverent in their behavior, not malicious gossips, nor enslaved to much wine, teaching what is good, that they may encourage the young women to love their husbands, to love their children, to be sensible, pure, workers at home, kind, being subject to their own husbands, that the word of God may not be dishonored.

But where are the younger women today? They are at their jobs, exactly where the older women, who have raised their families, have encouraged them to go, by their example. And now we hear of government subsidized National Child Care plans to further encourage parents to abandon their tiny children. This may enrich large corporations, since they will have a larger pool of cheaper labor to draw on, but will this kind of institutionalization lead to greater power and influence for Christianity?

What a powerful church we could have, and what strong families we could raise if only we women were doing *our* part and not trying to do the men's also! If the young woman not yet blessed with children would spend time helping the young mother, how much more prepared she would be when her own family came along. And how much the young mother could learn from the wisdom and experience of those women whose families have grown and started their own families!

Rick and I are convinced that my place is in our home, raising our blessings. After my relationship with my Lord, my husband and children are my top priority. Other opportunities are not allowed to conflict with my basic calling.

The world tends to view this attitude as narrow-minded and unsophisticated. They wonder how a woman confined within four walls, accompanied by numerous children, can have anything worthwhile to contribute to society.

Such a woman can certainly contribute something more valuable than a heated discussion on nuclear arms limitation or speculation on who's doing what to whom on the Hollywood scene. A woman fulfilling her role in the home will help her husband stand against the pressures of the outside world. And she is producing children who grow into honest, hardworking, godly adults who can lead a family, a company, or a nation.

As I walk down my "narrow-minded" path, doors of opportunities open for me on both sides along the way! I have the time to affect my family, my community, and my nation that women on a 9 to 5 schedule do not. They have time for a job; I have time for a *ministry*. I can comfort the afflicted, bake a casserole for a new mother, lobby my legislators by letter or phone, care for an elderly mother or sick child, create beautiful flower arrangements to refresh the spirits of our many visitors, or start a home business that will teach our children invaluable lessons of stewardship and leadership. The opportunities are limited only by my God-given priorities. As 1 John 5:3 says, "For this is the love of God, that we keep His commandments; and His commandments are not burdensome." Or, as Jesus said, "You shall know the truth and the truth shall make you free" (John 8:32). How I thank my children for needing me so much that I never got trapped in a "career" that would have eaten up the best hours of my day and the best years of my life. I still am a "working wife" at home — but I'm self-employed and free to serve others as much as I want!

I Can Do All Things Through Christ — By Myself I Can't Even Unclog the Toilet

One other comment I sometimes hear is, "You have eight children? I can't even handle the one(s) I have now!" My response is that I can't handle my eight either. I can't even handle my husband, or myself, let alone eight children! God does not expect us to raise children by ourselves. We must continually rely on Him for guidance, wisdom, and support.

I often remind myself that "children are a gift of the Lord; the fruit of the womb is a reward" (Psalm 127:3). Then I ask Him to help me treat His gifts as He wants me to treat them.

For more specific advice on Biblical child training, as well as suggested resources for further study, try Mary Pride's book *All the Way Home*. This book takes a management approach to child-training, as opposed to a therapeutic approach. For instance, Mary suggests we think in terms of *building team spirit* among our children rather than in terms of *dealing with sibling rivalry*. She also pinpoints the major (and often unseen) obstacles to child-training today and suggests steps to remove them.

You'll find that the real problem in raising children in late twentieth-century America (or England, or Australia, or Upper Volta) is that we are making things too hard on ourselves.

Naturally if you spend as little time as possible with your children, throw away the rod, forget to encourage their good behavior, and devour every tome written by the latest and greatest "parenting expert," you will have problems. So will you have problems if you let the kids hang around with every TV-trained neighborhood character, if you load them with money they haven't earned, and especially if you ship these little furnaces of undisciplined desires off on one of Satan's greatest thigh slappers — dates!

Let's stop trying to adjust our kids to American culture and start implementing Biblical principles in our families, and we'll have a lot less to worry about.

A Time for Every Purpose

Those of us seriously concerned about raising godly children often struggle with the problem of finding enough time. This might even be a reason in some women's minds for foregoing their complete quota of blessings. "How can I spend quality time with twelve kids?"

A mother of three told me that she wasn't sure if she wanted any more children. She felt it was very important to spend individual time regularly with each child. She had decided that if she had many children it would not be possible to have this personal time. It sounds logical: if you have twelve children, where will you find twelve hours every day to give each one individual time?

The desire for special time with each child sounds like a good excuse for not having a large family. But does it go along with the rest of Scripture? When we examine this argument closely, we see it is filled with the word *I:* "*I* want to spend individual time. *I* feel *I* can't do that with several children. *I* don't want any more children than *I* can handle. *I* am fulfilled and happy now." Shouldn't our main concern be with what God wants?

As we have tried to show in this book, God Himself is all the birth control we need. If He gives us children He will also give us time for them. May I repeat that? *If God chooses to give us children He will also give us the time for them!* We need only to be open and sensitive to His leading.

Remember Proverbs 3:5-6?

> Trust in the LORD with all your heart,
> And do not lean on your own understanding.
> In all your ways acknowledge Him,
> And He will make your paths straight.

Spending one-on-one time with our children is a worthy goal. As children of God we need to spend regular, uninterrupted time with Him. But just as it is possible for me to communicate with God throughout a busy day, I am able to give attention to the individual needs of our children throughout the day. That is, if I am willing to sacrifice my own time and desires.

There are many opportunities for focused time with our children throughout the day. Situations such as a skinned knee, a hard math problem, an exciting discovery in the yard, or some hurt feelings require and receive individual attention!

The time spent may not be half an hour, but important needs are met and personalized time is spent.

Rick mentioned our current plan for individualized attention in the last chapter. Each of us takes a child along when we go out. These excursions come up quite frequently. Then, too, there are all the unplanned special moments that occur throughout the day.

I want to add another important thought for those of you who now have small families. Remember when your parents told you, "You'll understand when you're older," and now you do? And remember when your married friends said, "You'll understand when you get married," and now you do? Well, you'll understand how this individualized time concept works as God enlarges your family!

Susanna Wesley did spend regular, individualized time with her nine surviving children (she also had two hours of private devotions every day). John had his hour with her on Thursday evenings. But unlike most modern mothers, she was also there to share all of the other moments of his day.

As we follow the principles of child training set down in His Word, God will show us how to get all the things done that He desires us to.

The Lessons of Pregnancy

Now that we have discussed the patience, organization, outside ministries, and time allocation, I would like to say something about childbearing itself.

Each of my pregnancies has brought its own joys and fears. Although I have never suffered a very troubled pregnancy, there was a chance of severe problems with our fourth child. We discovered this only eight weeks into the pregnancy, when our third child, Adam, contracted rubella and my immunity was found to be very low. After a series of blood tests over a period of several weeks, it was determined that there was probably no harm to the new child. Although the tests proved to be correct, the fears were still there until Stefani's birth. And I did suffer a miscarriage of our fifth child. I do know first-hand some of the fears and pains of troubled pregnancies. Had it not been for my Lord, my husband, my family and friends, these could have been devastating times.

As we were sharing about miscarriage and pregnancy one morning, a wise friend shared a thought with me. She had suffered two miscarriages and had learned much through them. She said that we have come to expect each pregnancy to produce a healthy child. But God may have *other* lessons for us to learn through pregnancy. Through the loss of a child or the birth of a child who is not quite "normal" according to our standards, God can teach us many things. We will learn, if we will be teachable, the importance of those little people whom God has chosen to be made after His image. We will learn to really lean on the God who longs for us to do so at all times. We will learn the importance of a loving husband, family, and friends. We will begin to really understand the importance of the qualities of compassion, sensitivity, responsibility, humility, loyalty, gratefulness, contentment, wisdom, faith, love, and security, just to name a few! Also, we will learn to truly be able to "Weep with those who weep."

Pregnancy is not easy for many women. But is that any reason to reject it? Should our attitude as Christians be, "If anything is too hard or inconvenient, don't bother with it"? Is that what God says? Does He want us to reject His revealed will because it may cause us some physical pain or emotional distress? Or should we embrace it as an opportunity to serve Him?

Pregnancy creates opportunities for Christian service even for women who are not pregnant. What an opportunity for the younger or older woman to serve the Lord by helping the soon-to-be-mom who gets ill at the *thought* of getting up out of bed! What a blessing to be able to serve a young mother who needs help with her house or toddlers because of her need to lie on the couch for nine months!

Some problems common to pregnancy can be dealt with easily. We can lose that extra weight and really get in shape before another child is conceived. We can eat properly and get as much rest as possible. We will look and feel better and say to the world, "God's gifts are worth having!"

How about this for a pregnancy verse? "Come unto me, all ye that labor and are heavy laden, and I will give you rest" (Matthew 11:28, KJV).

Sanctification Through Mothering

I know all mothers need rest!

Now, for the day-to-day grind, here is something beautiful to encourage you, from the pen of a noted theologian and father. Dr. H. Bavinck is about to point out how children can truly be a spiritual blessing to us:

> Children are the luxury of marital life, the treasure of the parents, the wealth of the family life. Their presence develops a great number of virtues in the parents, the father and mother—love, devotion and self-sacrifice, the care for the future, interest in the community, the art of education. Children check selfishness in parents, reconcile the contrasts,

soften the differences, bring the hearts of the parents ever closer to each other, give them a common interest that lives outside themselves, and opens their eyes and hearts to their surroundings and posterity. They uphold to the parents, as if in mirrors, their own virtues and defects, force them to reconsider their lives, soften their criticisms, and teach them how difficult it is to rule a human being. Out of the family life there proceeds a reforming power toward the parents. Who recognizes in the sensible, industrious father of a family the boisterous youth of former days, and who ever suspected the lighthearted maid of being changed, through her first-born, into a mother who willingly makes supreme sacrifices with cheerful patience? Family life turns the selfish into servants, misers into heroes, coarse men into considerate fathers, and tender mothers into courageous fighters. (Contained in J. Norval Geldenhuys, *The Intimate Life,* [Wheaton, IL: Eerdmans Publishing Company], 51, 52)

I will close with another wise thought from another dear friend: "God's grace is sufficient to enable His servants to carry out His principles!"

Believe it — act upon it — and be *blessed!*

Focus

- If you have children, what are the greatest concerns you have? How would having more children affect those concerns?

- Read a biography of Susanna Wesley.

- As you, a wife, imagine yourself with a larger family, do any of the following areas trouble you: organization, patience, societal pressure, outside ministry, priorities, time, and pregnancy? How does what has been discussed already help with these concerns?

11

SHOWERS OF BLESSING

W e are not only nearing the end of this book; we seem to be nearing the end of this age as well. As you and I look around us, we see how desperate is the hour and how great is the need.

While we thrill to reports from mission fields of the world, we must face facts. Never in two thousand years of church history have we found ourselves so far behind the world in terms of sheer numbers.

If the church was to be humanly graded as to how well its percentages have kept up with the world's, it may rate an *F*. Isn't that paradoxical in an age when we have the globe blanketed by Christian radio and have the most missionaries on the field the world has ever seen? (Quite a head-scratcher!) What *is* causing the church's lack of success?

The Problem

Today, Christians are fighting battles on several fronts. We face the issues of abortion, obscenity, the denial of parental rights in education, state gambling lotteries, infanticide, and enough other things to make a long and depressing list. Increasingly the government is acting in definitely anti-Christian ways.

Our Constitution was meant to provide stability in the midst of the changing whims of a self-indulgent society, but due to Constitutional redefinition that is no longer the case. The Constitution is no longer king. It is now just a piece of paper which means whatever a majority of the Chief Justices decides it means. It "evolves" to provide commentary for our pluralistic society. Instead of me rambling on forever, you would profit far more by reading *The Second American Revolution* by Christian legal expert John Whitehead (Crossway Books, 1984). It will be an eye-opener for anyone who imagines that American law is still based on the Constitution.

As John Adams stated to the Massachusetts militia in 1789, "We have no government armed in power capable of contending in human passions unbridled by morality and religion. Our Constitution was made only for a moral and religious people. It is wholly inadequate for the government of any other." We feel John Adams looking right at our day, watching us rapidly degenerate into an immoral and irreligious nation. It is not surprising that many don't appreciate the "restrictiveness" of the Constitution.

Today the Supreme Court justices are more important than the Constitution, and what is right or "legal" now depends on who is interpreting the Constitution at the time. In other words, in our own day the judicial branch of government has become the legislative.

Remember for a moment that the reason we have our backs to the wall and find ourselves a besieged *minority* is because we have let the world's humanistic thinking dictate our family sizes instead of allowing God to bless us with His provision.

In the early years of our country Christians, or people exemplifying Biblical morality, were the great *majority*.

Brethren, it's time for a comeback!

The Birth Dearth

Because we are going to be talking about populations and percentages, here is a report by the Census Bureau. It will give us some perspective on current situations and trends.

Americans had more children in 1984 than the previous year, but the surge in newborns was only an echo of the Baby Boom of the 1950s and early 1960s, the Census Bureau reported Sunday (July 21, 1985).

There were 3,690,000 births and 2,046,000 deaths in 1984, the Bureau said. In 1983 there were 3,618,000 births down from 3,681,000 in 1982. The report is the first since 1979 to analyze the components of population change.

In addition to the gain from births last year, net immigration was estimated at 523,000. That brought the nation's population to 237,839,000 as of Jan. 1, 1985.

There were 1,644,000 more births than deaths last year, but the new population increase did not result from a higher fertility rate, census officials said. Instead, it resulted from the fact that the children of the Baby Boom were having babies, the officials said.

In fact, the nation's total fertility rate for 1984 was 1,819 births per 1,000 women, which is below the level needed to keep the population constant.

Total fertility is defined by population experts as the number of children who would be born to 1,000 women during their lifetimes if the birth rate for a particular year remained unchanged in the future.

To keep the population constant, experts estimate a rate of 2,100 births per 1,000 women is necessary, to allow each woman to replace herself and her partner and to allow for some infant mortality.

Births are currently adding to the population because of the unusual number of people in the childbearing years. But as these people age, the smaller "Baby Bust" generation behind them will produce sharply fewer babies, if the rate remains the same, officials said.

Thus, if the total fertility rate remains low over a period of years, the population will eventually stabilize, and then could begin to fall as deaths begin to exceed births, experts say.

However, even with the assumption of ultimate fertility of 1.9 births per woman, it would take about 40 years for the population to stop growing, the Bureau advised.

The new study looked at three different measures of fertility, and found current activity well below Baby Boom levels in each category.

The total fertility rate of 1,819 per 1,000 women edged up from 1,791 per 1,000 in 1983, but was less than half the rate of 3,760 recorded in 1957 — when the Baby Boom peaked.

The total fertility rate dropped by 27 percent from 1970 to 1984, the Bureau reported.

To sum up the article, at present levels of childbearing, America will follow West Germany's lead and completely run out of people in a few hundred years. *The Birth Dearth* chronicles this in detail.

Not Enough Christians

Let's juggle some numbers around. At the time of this writing there are nearly 250 million people in the U.S. A poll taken a few years ago announced to the astonishment of many that approximately one out of three Americans surveyed claimed to be "born again."

Now let's talk turkey for a minute. Not to be negative, but 85 million believers in America?

When the results of the poll were published, it was mentioned that people from different cults called themselves "born again." Also, multitudes who were baptized as babies responded that they were born again also.

If there were truly 85 million new hearts in our nation, we wouldn't be able to recognize the place.

Let's whittle the number down, at least to 25 million active Christians. If A. W. Tozer was correct, that may still be very high, but at least it is closer. That is only ten percent of our whole country.

With that number as a starting place, here we are, marching into the 1990s, 25 million redeemed and 225 million not—quite a gap! If the Christian birthrate matches that of secular society, every year the numerical gap between believers and unbelievers will increase. Every year our influence will dwindle more and more, and the nation's ethics and morality will plummet even faster.

"In the Dearth of a People is a Prince's Ruin" (Proverbs 14:28)

Let's be as practical as possible. Take an objective look at the national scene. It is not pleasing to the Lord, and as we believers become an ever-smaller fragment of the population, the picture figures to darken still more. So, how can we influence our government for good? Pray and support candidates on all levels who have a Biblical foundation (or at least high moral convictions).

Anything else?

Well, how about *supplying* some of the candidates for office, leaders of corporations, heads of newspapers, Supreme Court judges, and butchers, bakers, and Indian chiefs?

Ah, here we have a problem. Where will we *get* them? And if we get them, will there be enough right-thinking support people to carry out their requests?

When at the height of the Reagan Revolution the conservative faction in Washington was enforced with squads of new conservative congressmen, these legislators often found themselves handcuffed by lack of like-minded staff. There simply weren't enough conservatives trained to serve in Washington in the lower and middle capacities. Even if some could get elected to office, they couldn't get their agenda implemented because there were *not enough people* ready to help them.

We have this problem of insufficient workers and leaders in other areas as well. In our home we are fortunate to get numerous monthly reports from mission agencies and individual missionaries. Most of you probably receive much missions-mail as well. If we take the time to synthesize all the various requests and needs, we discover that while many missionaries need funds, another often greater need is for people who will go. We hear that people in certain areas are *begging* for a missionary to come and teach them the things of God.

May we now suggest what the *root* problem is?

Arrows for the War

A family raising three or four children to follow Christ can have a great impact for Him. But what about a family raising nine for His glory?

Let's consider this — by having more children we can actually be contributing to world evangelism. Here are four facts:

1. Our children are the visible products of God's invisible will.

2. They are not truly our children — they are His property.

3. God has a revealed will concerning our children.

4. Part of that will involves training the children to be spiritual *soldiers!*

The Christian lives behind enemy lines. He is an "alien and stranger" (1 Peter 2:11). We must always strive to remember that we are not really at home here. We are at war. Now recall that one of the terms God uses for children is "arrows." The arrows of a warrior are not used for rototilling, kneading dough, or meteorology — they are weapons of war.

And what a warfare! Not physical, but unseen — spiritual. Ephesians 6:12 declares, "For our struggle is not against flesh and blood, but against the rulers, against the powers, against the world forces of this darkness, against the spiritual forces of wickedness in the heavenly places."

What can we glean from this? Simply that God had spiritual warfare in mind when He told the Psalmist that children were "arrows." And He has spiritual warfare in mind when He gives us children today.

Fruitfulness and Victory

If there are, say, 8 million Christian couples of childbearing age in the United States and they each have six children, that means that in twenty to thirty years those 16 million folks will have around 48 million children. Add that to the parents and we have 64 million people. If 90 percent of those 48 million children get married (according to our survey, 98 percent of singles hope for marriage) and the resulting 22 million couples each have six children, we arrive at a staggering 132 million children, which, when added to the previous generation (our kids), us, and some before equals around 200 million in 40-80 years. Some of us will return Home, so we'll pare it down to 190 million.

Can we go just one more generation? Given the same 90 percent and the same six children, and we get around 356 million births. Subtracting the rest of our generation and some of our children's gives us a total of around 550 million Christians still around (God does not promise that all of our children will be Christians, but we certainly see Him working that way very often in families) all in approximately a century, assuming Christ does not return before then. With the nation's low birth rate, the high divorce rate, an un-marrying and anti-child viewpoint, and a debauched nation perhaps unable to slow down the spread of AIDS, we can begin to see what happens politically. A half-billion person boycott of a company which violated God's standards could be very effective. And what a majority in elections the elect would enjoy. Whew — it's exciting! Through God's blessing we would be part of a replay of Exodus 1:7, "But the sons of Israel were fruitful and increased greatly, and multiplied, and became exceedingly mighty, so that the land was filled with them."

And we have quite an advantage which the Israelites did not: we can *vote*.

If the Body of Christ had been reproducing as we were designed and told to, we would not be in the mess we are today. It is a sad observation, but *none* of the social problems mentioned above would have surfaced if the Christian population was the five to ten times larger it could easily have been through God's blessing.

We are not trying to usher in Christ's kingdom in our country; that will not occur until He accomplishes it Himself. We must understand, though, that applying the principle of Christian fruitfulness can save us from becoming a voiceless fragment of our country in the near future.

Here is Walter Cronkite's great-grandson giving the election night returns from the November 6th, 2088 national elections: "Christians have captured the White House, 78 percent of the U.S. Senate, 85 percent of the House, and 44 gubernatorial races." Nice work! Social changes would inevitably come to pass, heralded by headlines like:

NFL OWNERS OPT FOR SATURDAY GAMES:
"Players Need Time for Church and Family on Sundays,"
Head Office Reports

HARVARD AND YALE RACE
TO HAVE FIRST ALL-CREATIONIST SCIENCE DEPTS.

SAN FRANCISCO PRONOUNCED SAFE
FOR HUMAN HABITATION

GM Unveils New Nine-Passenger Corvette!

As just one example of the clout God can give to a fruitful couple, we offer the legacy left by Jonathan and Sarah Edwards. In *The Value of Motherhood,* a booklet by Brenda Hunter, published by *Focus on the Family,* Mrs. Hunter makes reference to a study done by A. E. Winship in 1900, in which he lists some of the accomplishments of the 1,400 Edwards descendants he located. Winship says that,

> The Edwards family produced
> 13 college presidents,
> 65 professors,
> 100 lawyers and a dean of a law school,
> 30 judges,
> 66 physicians and a dean of a medical school,
> 80 holders of public office,
> three United States senators,
> mayors of three large cities,
> governors of three states,
> a vice president of the United States, and
> a controller of the United States Treasury.

Is it surprising that Jonathan Edwards remained the most influential New England theologian 100 years after his death, with all those descendants trained and ready to follow in his footsteps?

Workers for the Harvest

Now let's go on beyond politics to an even more promising area. Most readers have attended a missions conference at a church, Bible school, or seminary. Few things are so exciting or uplifting as hearing reports of God's amazing deeds in diverse areas of the world. While at one of these marvelous conferences, we've heard speakers quote Luke 10:2, "And He was saying to them, 'The harvest is plentiful, but the laborers are few; therefore beseech the Lord of the harvest to send out laborers into His harvest.' "

Here is a mild jolt — what about the very real possibility that God wants to use your marriage to send out *several* laborers into His harvest?

I am afraid that because of our addiction to birth control, many of the Lord's potential laborers haven't even made it into the *womb,* much less into the field. How tragic. Believing families of our day would do well to focus not so much on sending laborers into the harvest as on just harvesting some laborers.

It is amazing that I have never heard a missions leader castigate the church for choosing to limit world evangelism through limiting its families. The truth is that a believer who, after studying through this issue, still opts to engineer his own family, cannot say he is seriously concerned with world evangelism, especially since the most obvious way to raise more missionaries is to raise more godly children. This creates quite an enigma, summed up by this little limerick:

> A strange group are we, Evangilical,
> So backward in matters Umbilical;
> "The world we must win!",

But so few next of kin,
Makes our statement at best Hypocrilical.

20/20

Now let's start thinking with *vision*. God could honor your family by allowing it to have a significant part in the fulfillment of the "Great Commission" (Matthew 28:19, 20). Since we all need to develop God's perspective — His vision — perhaps you could develop your own letterhead; something to give a growing family a sense of destiny and purpose. Some examples might be:

- The Davis World Outreach Association

- The Stearn Center for Advanced Missions Studies

- The Presley Consortium for the Building of International Harvesters

At a future missions conference you may hear a speaker proclaim the famous troika of opportunities, "You can pray; you can give; you can go!" After adding an optional "Amen," it would be every bit as accurate to stand up and boldly say, "And you can *reproduce!*" (Please write and send us your church's reaction to this tactic.)

How to Grow a Church

Speaking of missions, let's speak of the church — your church. The church is being inundated by scads of books, seminars, and so forth on how to get a bigger church. How strange that in all the high-priced opinions everyone misses quite a large part of the boat.

Consider a hypothetical First Church. Over at First they have forty young married couples. Let's assume that they all read this book or study the Bible on this subject and decide to trust God to do the best for them in their family size. Let's assume too that God gives each couple eight children. So now we have 320 children, plus the original eighty parents, equalling 400 people (better plan on much bigger youth departments). Supposing that God has singleness for one out of every eight, and that of the 280 kids who marry, 100 marry within the church family, we end up with 230 couples.

Now this new generation has been taught well, sees the manifold blessings God has graced their parents with (they really love their brothers and sisters too!), and decides to trust God for their families. God blesses their faith by giving each couple eight children. And presto! They have 1,840 children. Add that to the 320 of the previous generation, plus forty grandparents (half have gone Home to a *great* reward) and our original forty couples have become 2,200 people just two generations later!

In just one more generation, using the same percentage (one in eight not marrying), and 500 marrying within the circle of their church friends, an eight-fold blessing by God will yield 10,880 children, plus 1,840 parents, 160 grandparents, and ten remaining great-grandparents. This makes a most attractive total of 12,890 people — all from just the young marrieds' group three generations earlier. And we can add to that the numbers won to Christ through the lives of these people. Believers who've discovered they can trust God for their families may just witness much better than those who feel they can't or won't! First Church's directory would be bigger than the phone books for most of our Nebraska cities.

More Vision, This Time for You Wives

Now, as you are reading this you may have just had a horrendous day with a toddler or two in diapers, causing you to wish you had taken a vow of celibacy years ago. Sit down, cool off, and let's peer into a delightfully possible future of yours.

Picture this — you are fellowshipping with a group of older ladies on a Sunday afternoon on a sunny veranda. You're sipping lemonade and the conversation turns to what "the children" are doing. Mrs. X says, "Oh, my John is a pastor!" Mrs. Y chimes in with, "My Archibald teaches in a Bible College." Others list things their children are currently involved in. Now it's your turn. Sit up straight and smile as you begin, "Well, Jack is a missionary in Yugoslavia; Jill works with her husband as a Bible translator in Antarctica; Bill, his wife, ·nd their seven children are church planters in the Hudson Бay area; Janice is discipling young women in Vladivostok; Abigail works at a Christian radio station in the Middle East with her husband and their five children; Mezuzah (you and your Bible names!) and his wife head an indigenous work on one of the Martian mining colonies. It's quite a story how God provided space suits for their eleven little ones! And Joseph is a car mechanic on 14th Street. He has two Bible studies going for the men he works with and brings one of his six boys to work with him on Fridays. I don't remember what all his girls do." Go ahead — have another sip of lemonade — you've earned it! And now finish, "Paul, Timothy, and Titus are still shepherding churches and helping their wives educate their children at home. All sixteen of them."

Bravo! If God gives you ten children they may not all be spiritual dynamos, but if you raise them relying on God and His Word and have given them the gigantic head start of knowing that you trusted Him for their births, why expect less?

The first ten chapters were aimed at you, the individual. This chapter has its sights set on the church, in a national and even a global scope. The political blessings of Christian fruitfulness are invigorating to ponder and plan, but the missionary blessings are overwhelming. What a missionary force we could send! And the financial blessings possible from a vast number of giving Christians are enormous. Imagine if corporations, then headed by Christians, switched their tax-deductible contributions from funding the Mesopotamian Coastal Drum and Bugle Corps to funding missions organizations.

Let us pray and ask the Lord of the harvest to use our own families to raise up a host of dedicated young men and women who will serve Him anywhere. Then we can all quote Luke 10:2 with a clear conscience.

Jan and I pray that you may be positively challenged with such extremely possible scenarios. The world will never know what hit it. But we will, for our God will have done it.

May the future testimony of our children's generation of young Christians be Psalm 105:24:

> *And He caused His people to be very fruitful,*
> *And made them stronger than their adversaries.*

Focus

- What might the United States be like today, had the last three generations of godly believers averaged seven children, rather than two and a half, assuming the missing children were trained up in the things of God?

- In this chapter we looked at a hypothetical 2088 election return, and a blessed method of church growth based on the church becoming willing to let God be God. But how does it work on a smaller scale?
  Suppose you are given eight children and seven of them marry. Each of these couples is given eight children, of which seven marry. And the same holds true for the next generation. How many birthday cards will you be sending out to your children, grandchildren, their spouses, and your great-grandchildren? Could make for a wonderful Mother's Day! Now *that's* a heritage!

- How excited might Satan be at the prospect of the Bride of Christ being truly fruitful and multiplying?

APPENDIX A

HEADS OR TAILS—GOD OR PROBABILITY?

A s we travel through life, we find from time to time
things we have accepted as being true which, upon
closer examination, are less than accurate.

For example, in matters religious, one may believe that they
were "always a Christian," or became one when someone sprin-
kled water on their newborn noggins, or when they were con-
firmed, or dozed through their first sermon. When we are truly
saved and study the Scriptures, we understand differently.

In other areas, people may believe that the shadow of the
earth causes the effect of the crescent moon, universities are
benevolent centers of wisdom, cottage cheese is produced by
people jumping barefoot in huge vats of milk in Southern
France (please don't laugh—it's embarrassing enough), and
human reproduction is governed by probability.

What we have learned is that the crescent moon is a function of the sun's position, universities are fundamentally
places where one can spend many years and many more thousands of dollars for the privilege of being filled with untruths
and emptied of morals, and that cottage cheese is made by

people jumping barefoot in huge vats of milk in *Northern* France. But what was that last one? Human reproduction isn't governed by probability?

Before tackling that one, we must become amateur anthropologists, considering types of cultures or societies. Cultures tend to precipitate nicely into one of two types. Some cultures think of themselves as scientific and rational while others are non-scientific and non-rational (it's always the scientific/rational types that provide the labels). A non-rational society is likely to attribute things and events they experience to a spiritual force or set of spiritual forces. A mechanistic culture assumes natural causes and therefore rational explanations for everything. That seems to be where the industrialized West is with regard to a great many things (of note is the fact that the New Age movement could make the West the first macro-culture to be both technologically advanced and non-rational comfortably). The West has lost its use for God and so too its use for true Christianity partly because its rational/materialist scientists and philosophers have figured everything out, or assure us they're close, or at the very least they tell us they are sniffing down the right rut. Plain ol' USDA Grade A Non-Fancy Humanism, of course, but a comforting thought, because we in the U.S. are a nation of knowers—we want to know everything about everything.

Let's examine what our scientists, philosophers, and educators believe and teach about human reproduction. They would give us what we might call The Seven Deadly Axioms. More could be listed, but these seven will be a sufficient base from which to examine our reproductive thinking. They are:

1. If you have green eyes and your spouse has brown eyes, there is an X percent chance that your children will have brown eyes.

2. A couple has a one-in-four chance of being barren.

3. A woman will experience menopause near age fifty.

4. If your grandparents or parents had twins, you have a greater chance to duplicate the feat than do others.

5. Women over forty have a much greater chance of delivering a baby with a birth defect.

6. If unprotected intercourse occurs around fourteen days after the onset of a woman's period, there is a good chance that conception will result.

7. A mother-to-be's due date is 280 days after the start of her last period.

Speaking for Jan and myself, the above statements are accurate reflections of our thinking until not very long ago.

Understanding the nature of probability and then examining its logical conclusions in the believer's thinking and decision making is crucial before we embark on such an easily-misunderstood journey.

The words "probability" and "probably" come from "probable," which is derived from the Latin *probabilis*. The primary root is *probo* — to prove. Today, when we say "probable" we mean that not only might a thing happen, it's likely to take place. That's acceptable and we have no bones to pick with the concept. But when we begin to make major life decisions based on probability, we skate on improbably thin ice. We want to scrutinize the seven axioms (truths considered so self-evident as to require no outside corroborative evidence) listed above to find how really "self-evident" they are and especially how much influence they should exercise in the believer's thinking. They are the sort of ideas which lobby us hard for a certain view of human reproduction and genetics; namely, that they are essentially functions of probability. Here is the first of the etched-in-stone axioms:

Axiom 1

If I have green eyes and my spouse has brown
(easy for Jan and I to imagine), there is
an X percent chance that our children
will have brown eyes.

This "law" seems sound enough, but to introduce a tiny question: where is God in it?

Well, He set up the laws and now lets them run their own course, such that it is statistical probability's job to decide everything from when life will arise to how many freckles the life will have. So, probability has been granted a gargantuan promotion; it has become deity, thereby earning the status of a philosophy or a religion, in the same way that Evolution or Natural Selection has. For example, we are familiar with phrases such as, "Evolution chose the white winter coat for the snow-shoe rabbit." And in the same way, the laws of probability (for probability is a law-giving deity) mandate and control eye color proportions in a family or race.

Trouble is, God proves over and over that He opens and shuts the womb and that He, not statistics (probability's brother), is the One responsible for designing us while we were yet embryonic. So, for the Christian there is a question of enormous importance — we see God and probability, heads or tails. Only one side can land up. It is essential that we know which it is — or should be. In terms of our first axiom, does God decide eye color or does Mendel's Law?

We would all agree that it is ultimately God who is in control — the thorny question is then how much control does "ultimately" imply? If we assign all causative functions to God, what are we to do with probability, statistical trends, and genetics? Isn't it true, after all the theological theorizing is through, that if both of my parents had blue eyes I will probably have blue eyes?

It all depends. The whole probability issue revolves around time, and not in an abstract, relativistic way. To provide a very brief explanation, here is a little 300-words-or-less essay on probability. Perhaps it could be helpful in modifying our outlook on having babies.

Probability

Probability is the branch of mathematical science which deals with the likelihood of an event's occurrence. Considered from a Biblical mind-set, it is capable of performing just one function: it can describe how God has worked in the past. A corollary to that is that probability has absolutely no ability to predict what God will do in the life of an individual in the future.

God could, from this moment on, give every offspring of every four blue-eyed marriage in the world brown eyes. He would not be doing anything wrong or even irrational, for probability again has no prophetic powers. It cannot foretell, much less dictate, anything in the future. God has never bound Himself to any "law" concerning the design of living

things, save one, things reproduce after their own kind—
Genesis 1:29—and that has reference only to specielization
(species).

Again, though, we're bound to point out, "But just look at
all those blue-eyed couples with blue-eyed kids!" Okay, let's
look. One would certainly agree that in that situation, blue-
eyed children are what we've tended to see. What we also
see is the correct use of probability. That is probability functioning descriptively *in the past tense.* We can be very comfortable affirming "83.56 percent of the children with blue-
eyed parents have blue eyes themselves." But, to grant to
probability the apparent immutability of a natural law like
gravity is not in the least accurate, valid or scientific. Probability gave none of those children blue eyes. God did. God
individually chose and gave to each child his or her blue
eyes. We have to keep in mind that God can modify or abol-
ish genetic or reproductive past trends as He wills.

Perhaps a name change could help us. Let's try renaming
the Law of Probability: "The Observed Past Workings of
God" (OPWOG). Now we are free to allow God to be the
selective and determinative molder of individuals He presents Himself to be.

We will discover differences between probability and
OPWOG by comparing them in the other six axioms.

Axiom 2
*A couple has a one-in-four chance
of being barren.*

A couple contemplating marriage may see this statistic and be
apprehensive, fearful, or see a lifetime of substituting pets for

progeny, although more and more it must be agreed that the prospects of a childless union may be viewed favorably by couples steeped in the errors of the day. Assuming that our young engaged couple does want children, must not such a barren pronouncement cause fear or anxiety? But Paul told the Philippian church, "Be anxious for nothing" (4:6).

"Well, it was easy for him to say that — he didn't understand modern fertility rates and statistics like we do. He didn't know there was a one-in-four chance that we will not be able to have children."

The real reason Paul could make such a strong statement was due to his concept of God. He knew that God's control is infinite in breadth and depth (including human reproduction) and his faith had not been squashed by the misapplication of twentieth century statistical genetics like mine has been. Paul's response to axiom 2 may have been rather scathing.

Biblically, barrenness may be the direct work of God for purposes of a curse, as per Abimelech in Genesis 20:17-18: "And Abraham prayed to God; and God healed Abimelech and his wife and his maids, so that they bore children. For the LORD had closed fast all the wombs of the household of Abimelech because of Sarah, Abraham's wife." (A modern-day example of barrenness as a curse is found in *The Pineapple Story,* published by the Institute in Basic Life Principles, 1978.)

Barrenness may also be no more than a question of timing — a Divine "Not Yet," as it were. Again, Abraham and Sarah come to mind. She was never in her life barren *in the sense of being sterile* — God was only waiting for the proper time to accomplish Isaac's conception. There is a mammoth difference between "never" and "not yet." I would not have wanted to be the gynecologist responsible for telling Sarah

and Abraham, "Well, tough luck folks. You're one of the unlucky one-in-four. My recommendation is that you find a sur-
rogate mother." Enter Hagar. We should consider also the Divine delay in Rachel's time of childbearing. It was God, not
probability, who was waiting for the right time to open her
womb.

Fertility is entirely and absolutely the work of God. The
correct response to axiom 2 is that there is 100 percent
"chance" that a marrying couple will be barren, or there is a
100 percent "chance" that they will not. And then there are the
100 percent barrens who miraculously are turned into 100 percent parents. Here is an amazing and moving story a godly
young couple told to our fellowship recently. We asked if they
would consent to have it printed in this book, as it will be so
encouraging to those who have had a reproductive *death sentence* passed on them. They sent this to us.

> We used birth control (diaphragm) for the first two years of
> our marriage. Our desire was to wait to have children until
> my husband was out of school.

> During those years we talked of having three children and
> spacing them about two years apart. Also during that time I
> committed a few things to God in prayer. The first was that
> if our children would not grow up to honor and serve God, I
> asked the Lord not to give them to us. I couldn't (and still
> can't) imagine anything more painful than giving birth to a
> child and then have that child spend eternity apart from
> God. The second was a submission that if God wanted to
> give us handicapped children, that was okay with me—I'd
> try to learn and submit in that area also.

> When my husband's surgery (in October of 1984, two years
> and two months after we were married) led to a diagnosis of
> testicular cancer, I did a lot of reading about his disease and

its effects on fertility. The *literature* stated that most men could still father children after the surgery (in which one testicle was removed) and the radiation therapy (from which the other testicle was *mostly* shielded). So, when the urologist suggested we check into a sperm bank before treatments began, I didn't really see the need. As my husband and I talked it over, we decided *no*. I (having grown up on a farm) correlated artificial insemination with cows and am too much of a *romantic* to thrill at the thought of getting pregnant in a doctor's office with the bright lights, rather than . . . well, you know! We also decided to let God have control in that area of our lives!

Well, my husband had his seven weeks of radiation therapy and from his surgery on, we used no form of birth control. One year after completing his treatments I went to the doctor and had a physical with some blood tests and began charting my basal body temperature. There were no fertility problems detected in me. So, we scheduled a postcoital exam. I'm sure you've heard of them — what humiliation! At that exam my doctor was checking the quality of the vaginal mucous as well as for antibodies to the sperm, but low and behold: He didn't see any sperm. So, our next course was a sperm count. I'm not sure, but I think a normal sperm count is twenty to sixty million. When my husband's was checked he had ten—not ten million, but only ten sperm, and eight of them were not viable (dead) and the other two were immature. So, the urologist told us we had about a zero percent chance of getting pregnant. I quit taking basal temps and we left it in God's hands. The sperm count has never been rechecked.

June of 1986 is when we moved and I was ready to take on motherhood, but I wasn't pregnant and everyone knows how long adoption procedures take. I went through a bit of depression at that time, but we began checking into adoption and foster care of children. Well, it was early December of that year when I found out I was pregnant. We were thrilled and had many opportunities to share with believers and unbelievers about God's faithfulness to us! About seven weeks later I miscarried and everything came crashing in around me. But God was still faithful and we still had many opportunities to share that with people. Many well-meaning friends assured us that I'd get pregnant again right away, and my hopes were high, but as the months wore on I became quite angry with God and went through some *real* depression. I felt like God had dangled a baby in front of me like dangling a carrot in front of a starving rabbit. I also was not open to adoption any longer. I wanted MY baby! It took about a year for me to work through all of that and once again we began to pursue adoption. So, January of 1988 was when I wrote to an adoption agency and in April we discovered again that I was pregnant. It was a scary time — afraid of giving ourselves to it emotionally. Afraid of the hurt and disappointment of losing another child. But, in God's timing, Gregory was born December 12, 1988!

We have enjoyed parenthood more than I ever dreamed possible, and as an *infertile* couple, we had pretty high dreams. At this point in my life I can't ever imagine not wanting to have another baby. We are trusting God for the size and timing of our family and really do look forward to seeing what He has in store for us.

We have no idea if my husband has been healed or if God has just opened my womb to allow us to have conceived the now two children we have, but we continue to grow in confidence of His sovereignty in this area of our lives."

What a story! What a powerful, loving God we serve!

Truly, God is the Author of life and it is His decision, not probability's sperm counts, that will determine whether or not there are to be children. Though concealed from our now-bound vision, He only deals in sure things.

Axiom 3
A woman will experience menopause
near age fifty.

Our friend Connie might like to respond to that; her grand-mother began menopause at age 39. You may know women who also began much earlier or later than 50. "But it's usually around 50." Granted, it has been — in the past only — OPWOG. There have likely been differences in the average age at which menopause began in different generations, according to God's purposes. A rhetorical question: does God control menopause? Is He its Initiator and Concluder? An affirmative answer means that God will bring about menopause when He deems it best and end it for the same reason. In truth, given that God controls the onset of menopause as well as the giving of children, all mystery about menopause vanishes. Menopause occurs at exactly the time in a woman's life when God decrees that she is to bear no more children. To those who stand aghast at the thought of a never-ending string of pregnancies, be encouraged! You will certainly hear "You will have no more children" and it could be spoken no more loudly or clearly than by God's closing the curtain on your fertility. Aside from mechanistic theories, no other plausible explanation for God's purpose in menopause fills the bill — menopause marks the time a couple should cease expecting God to bless them with children. For most today it is a relief — for a few, however, a time of sadness and a sense of deep loss.

Having a fully God-stocked quiver when God initiates menopause will be a great comfort, though.

Women who say they will undergo menopause at age fifty are making a bold statement. Can we know when God will do anything without some revelation from Him? Or, in the parlance of my early Christian life, "Chapter and verse!" God has planned the perfect time in each woman's life to initiate menopause. Again, probability can only try to say what has been the collective average of God's workings in individual lives. That's the trouble — you are all wonderfully individual and are handled, cared for, and loved individually and uniquely by your loving Father. Therefore, "fifty" is a nearly useless number in the life of a Christian woman. God will end the fertile portion of your life just like He started it — at any time He chooses!

As an aside, let's not be surprised to find someday in glory that God has given His daughters of this and the next generation more childbearing years than others — especially in these times, when the church (Jan and I included) has played the rube so ruinously for years. God may, most graciously, allow our generation and our daughters' to play a major role in catching up.

Axiom 4
*If your grandparents or parents had twins,
you have a greater chance to duplicate them
than do others.*

Translation: "If God gave your predecessors twins, He will be more likely to give you twins than He is to give others twins." Isn't that true? We know instances in which an older couple had twins and then their children, or children's children did as well.

Let us review the points we are making in this chapter by the ever-helpful practice of making clear what we are *not* saying. First, we are not saying that probability has chosen multiple births for one family and then done the same for that family's descendants. Friends, probability could not be more dead. It is entirely dead. It has no power, ability, or will to choose anything. It is only and at most a descriptive tool for those in the present tense to cast backwards and attempt to measure things in the past tense. Sometimes it works well and sometimes not.

Nor are we maintaining that the DNA structure of our cells cannot contain the requisite genetic material for multiple births if our grandparents' did or that it could contain more of the mechanism associated with twins than might others without twins in their near past.

What we *are* aiming at is this — it may be close to blasphemous (that is, God-denying) to hold that because our parents had twins we will probably have twins. Once again, statistics is not what controls our births, be they single or multiple. God chooses the perfect number of children to bless us with in each pregnancy. If He chooses to use genetic material in the DNA molecule to cause twins to be born, it is still His choice for that particular family at that particular time for that unique pregnancy. Probability is left with an exquisite involvement percentage of zero.

God does not act out of statistical necessity — "Michael, we've had 6,562 conceptions today. How many sets of twins are scheduled? Only one?? Split that egg in two and assign an extra angel to the case!"

The analogy that has been helpful to us in this matter of God and DNA is that of the artist with his palette. The artist has a number of colors arranged on the palette. He may choose to use those or he has the option of mixing them or even adding new colors to his creation if he desires. The DNA molecule is wondrously complex and we do not yet fathom its workings in great detail. I recently heard a geneticist say that as far as anyone knew, 60 percent of our DNA coding is useless "junk." God being the architect of the DNA double helix, the junk theory appears to be aptly named. Even if some couple has more DNA material associated with multiple births than others, that material must still be chosen and activated by God if twins or triplets are to be born. Similarly, God may, if He wishes, choose to give twins to a family that does not have a record of them in the parents or grandparents.

This is not a simple issue of semantics. Dethroning probability and crowning God as the Prime Factor in all matters of reproduction will cause us to lose fear and apprehension concerning many areas related to God's control of our family size.

Axiom 5
Women over forty have a greater chance of having a baby with a birth defect.

This is the most chilling of all the axioms. It may have prevented more women from trusting God for a child after a certain age than any other single factor. A child with a birth defect breaks our hearts and can cause major changes in a family, altering the schedule and even lifestyle of the other members. Yet our real need, once again, is to understand the fundamental principles behind the statements.

Initially, the axiom again resurrects blind chance. Now it has donned a mask of hideous ugliness. The question is not one of having a child with blue versus hazel eyes; the issue is an abnormal life. Chance is posed as an evil second only to the Grim Reaper and only marginally better (given the exhibited tendency through abortion to melt or hack to death "defective" children before birth or starve them after, it seems that to some death ranks as a morally superior alternative).

Secondarily, as we saw in the quote from chapter six, there is evidence now pointing to an exhilarating possibility: that over-40 moms may not be at greater "risk" (there we go again) after all. With probability a key thing to keep in mind is that statistics can always be skewed as much as 180 degrees, as may have been the case here all these years.

Nonetheless, mothers of all ages have babies with birth defects. Surely we cannot lay the blame on God for this, can we? Explore two alternatives:

- Statistics — maybe probability *is* an actual entity and makes randomized evil choices in genetics.

- The introduction of system-damaging factors. It is known that use of drugs, alcohol, and smoking during pregnancy (especially the first trimester) may be detrimental to the developing infant.

But doesn't that second one put chance back at the wheel and God in the back seat? Isn't that the opposite of all that has been laid out in this appendix?

Not at all. Through the entire gestation process God is still the Divider of cells and Former of organs. If contaminants are introduced into the immediate environment of a little life, there are no ill effects unless God allows them. He may and at times obviously does allow them. The balance is that there is still cause and effect—but God is continually cognizant and absolutely in control of every factor coming to bear on the new life at every moment. We may speak in our ignorance of an X percent chance of damage to a preborn due to, say, an overexposure of x-rays, but in God's sight there is no "chance." It is absolutely "will" or "won't." The God of our Bible is not a spectator, wringing clammy hands and watching to see if the cell division will go awry at a crucial point in a pregnant mother foolish enough to drink. He will accomplish His will, and it will be perfect.

David addresses the question of genetic "malfunctions" in Psalm 139:13: "For Thou didst form my inward parts; Thou didst weave me in my mother's womb."

Is God therefore responsible for birth defects? A valid question. An answering question might be, does He or does He not preside over every millisecond of the entire process of gestation? If not, we are obligated to determine how often He "checks in," daily, hourly, perhaps monthly, like an OB. Theoretically He is perhaps always watching, but adopts a "hands-off" policy. No, these cannot be true, for we have just seen that He is the weaver of our babies, the bright Hope for the expectant mother. He is omnipresent with each child at every point in time. We would be in miserable straits were He to let random chance take over the development of a soul meant for eternity.

Could Psalm 139 apply to dysfunctional livers, three-chambered hearts, and minds with only half the capacity to learn? "A loving God would never make a child with a deformity!" would be the sentiment of some. The truth is clearly set forth in God's own words to Moses: "And the LORD said to him, 'Who has made man's mouth? Or who makes him dumb or deaf, or seeing or blind? Is it not I, the LORD?'" (Exodus 4:11).

Jan and I must share our testimony here.

In 1975 God gave us our first child, Staci, and she suffered from a severe birth defect. Then Andromeda was born two years later and there was another grave birth defect. It could be considered amazing or just plain stupid that we have continued to have children, since each of our eight has a serious birth defect. The birth defect that each of our children has tops any list of birth defects. The defect afflicting every one of our children and infecting our entire family is the sin nature.

We do not speak facetiously. Claiming that Down's Syndrome is even remotely as tragic as a child's innate sinfulness is not being realistic. Down's Syndrome does not cause lying. It does not cause stealing. It does not lead to fornication and consequently to the spread of venereal disease and AIDS. It does not destroy marriages. It does not promote greed, or lead to murder. It does not fit a soul for eternal judgment. Man's depravity is a horrid well of wickedness, so reprehensible that words cannot paint a picture black enough to depict all the ills, grief, and sorrow caused by this most heinous of all birth defects. And yet here we find an amazing thing — every single person created by God will suffer from and cause others to suffer from the nature of sin and He knows it too well; not simply that a little one He is weaving has a sin nature, but also every act of sin he or she will ever commit and how much grief they may bring to their parents, friends, future spouse, children, and His church. No matter how desperately we want to believe that God is incapable of playing a part in bringing a physically marred child into existence, we must deal with one great realization: He does, indeed, knowingly

and willingly bring forth spiritually crippled children. Every
baby born into the world is entirely fashioned by God and has
the greatest and most tragic birth defect imaginable. Dear
friend, God will never give us anything but His absolute best
for us, no matter what our age.

Axiom 6

*If unprotected intercourse occurs around fourteen
days after the beginning of a period, there is a
good chance that conception will result.*

"O, lamentable chance!" may be a phrase many would borrow
from Shakespeare to express this axiom. When the saints find
the above has occurred to them, the exclamation better suited
would be a hearty "Hallelujah!" (it has taken years for me to
make the transition from not feeling the former to actually
being able to honestly say the latter).

Fundamentally, there is not a problem with this axiom.
God has certainly designed our systems in such a way and
given us detailed instructions as to how best to optimize them
to allow Him to bless us with conception (see pages 116–118).
There are two distasteful parts of the axiom, however; "unprotected" here is shorthand for "unprotected from the blessing of
God." God's blessing doesn't seem like something to be protected from. The phrase "good chance," provides fresh opportunity to stick another sword in probability's belly.

In this axiom we are face-to-face once again with a dead,
randomized vision of life. We are the only sentient factors in
this axiom, so it is our non-Divine calling to take the bull by
the horns and protect ourselves lest God bless us, and not for

sneezing. A fatalistic view of life this is, and far from correct doctrine and right living.

"A good chance conception will result" is another example of the type of thinking common to us. Now, from our vantage point it may seem like there is a real good "chance," and as we know from OPWOG we may say that in 72 percent of the cases in which our axiomatic criteria are met, pregnancies have resulted. But here's the kicker: dare we say that *we* have a 72 percent "chance" of becoming pregnant? Not if there is a living God, we don't.

Perhaps rendering the truth mathematically will be helpful to us. Here is how the world sees conception: sperm + egg = Life. Ah, but here is how we know it to be: (sperm + egg) ^{God} = Life. (Sperm plus egg by the power of God yields Life!) Our "chances" are either a thundering 100 percent Yes! (yee-haw!) or a silent 100 percent No (rats!).

Axiom 7
A woman's due date is 280 days after the start of her last period.

A question not liable to pop up in your next game of Trivial Pursuit is: how many women have babies *on* their due date? After virtually no exhaustive research, the answer can now be revealed — the great majority. This may be less than earth-shattering, but Moms, for the enormous majority of you ("enormous" not being the greatest adjective to use when speaking of a pregnant woman) the day your baby is born is your due date! That's a fun thought, though not cover material for *The New England Journal of Medicine.* Mothers-to-be, your "due date" is not 280 days from the start of your last period. That figure is only a rough average based on how the Observed Past Workings Of God Are Kicked Into the Future By Those Who Generally Do Not Acknowledge Him—OPWOGAKIF-BTWGDNAH—a spurious postulate of OPWOG and a downright horrible word to try to pronounce.

While not as far reaching as the other axioms, this really helps the wife who frets, "I'm six days past my due date!" No you're not, ma'am—you're likely right on time with nothing to worry about. Jan always(!) delivers past her "due date." I've kidded her about trying to mimic the twenty to twenty-two month gestation period of the elephant. Amazing is the only word that can describe how well she hides her amusement. She has this anecdote to relate about "always" delivering past her due date.

Recently, my friend Jane had a beautiful baby boy. I went to the hospital with another friend, Laura, to see mother and son. The new child's statistics were being discussed and it was pointed out that he "will have blue eyes." Laura agreed, adding that all of her children will also have blue eyes. I mentioned the god of probability and carried on a pretty good argument for the sovereignty of God. Then I turned to Laura and said, "You are next," meaning she would have the next baby. She said "not necessarily!" Laura and I have due dates for our upcoming deliveries three days apart. I argued, "You always deliver pretty much on time and I always deliver late." Laura and Jane both laughed—they had me, and they were right. Just because I deliver "late" and Laura delivers near her given "due date" does not mean that she will deliver her baby before I deliver mine. Many years of probability are hard to rout out of a person's life!

Amen, Jan! Both of us are learning just how ingrained in us the "law of probability" is. But we are learning. We know now just to smile at each other when her "due date" is calculated. Then, when it's time to pick a week for vacations at work, I say, "I'd like any week in this six week period off," and try to smile sheepishly.

Jan writes again, three days before Zachary's birth:

This very situation has become real to us as we await the birth of our eighth child. Early in my pregnancy I had an ultrasound giving me a due date of May 27th. But I knew that my 280 day date was June 1st.

This was just an interesting difference until the May 27th date was passed by fourteen days. Suddenly, the baby and I were at "high risk." I have mentioned to my doctor three times that the ultrasound date is impossible. He maintains that this date is accurate to within plus or minus 3 days of delivery. Because we follow the abstinence principles laid out in chapter six, the ultrasound date has me pregnant two to eight days before I could have conceived. As an average, God has delivered our other children on the 290th day (today is day 291!).

By the way, finding a physician or qualified midwife who understands the principles we've been talking about is a great comfort.

There is a good deal of repetition in the treatment of our Seven Deadlies. I think all of us need it. We have been waffled by decades of "If this, then an X percent chance of this." It's all very logical and it all reeks, being the logic by which the church has been led to suffocation. The doctrine is inane, mundane, and insane. At the risk of belaboring the point, if we will just simply follow God's ways, He *will* give us the perfect number of children for our families. Ah — what relief!

As we have seen in this and other parts of this book, God controls every aspect of our reproduction; from hair and eye color, to the number of children a pregnancy will yield. We read this and yet we have already known it in our hearts. Our trouble is only that we are so inundated by all of society's randomized views of reproduction that we have a hard time preventing some of it from slipping into our thinking. Because God governs genetics absolutely, the words "chance," "possible," "might," and "probably" should be erased from our reproductive vocabularies. We are His children and, wonderfully, our Father has never uttered the word "probably." Our genetic percentages are always 100 percent and though the direction in which the 100 percent points is typically hidden from us, the God who loves us, plans and prepares our children for us, and works for our best does—and *that* is a truth we can rest in. We are too precious to God for Him to leave us to chance.

Life is not a running through the gauntlet, pummeled by one chance situation after another. We exist in God's ordered and principled universe and He deals with us individually, not as members of some statistical set, but as His unique children.

When we realize how utterly dead probability is with respect to the present or future, we come to an astonishing realization: *We have been held captive by a dead kidnapper.*

SURVEY OF CHRISTIAN ATTITUDES TOWARD FAMILY SIZE

D uring the writing of this book, we felt that it would be useful to do a survey for the purpose of discovering what factors influence the Christian in choosing what to believe and ultimately what to practice relative to family size.

We wanted to address specific areas of concern to Christians; areas that were causing believers to feel the need to take control of the number and spacing of their children.

Realistically, the populace as a whole is not enamored with statistics. That being the case, many of you will have more use for your own appendix than for ours. No problem. This section is for those who are interested in discovering how many children the twenty-year-olds plan on having or how money affects desire for children.

The surveys were prepared and given to four evangelical churches (Berean, Christian and Missionary Alliance, Evangelical Free, and General Conference Baptist) and one Bible College. Three of the church surveys were done in Sunday School settings with the fourth done on a Wednesday evening, by the helpers in a large church youth program. We were very pleased by the spread of ages, situations, and backgrounds represented by the 253 people who filled out the questionnaires.

Displaying a questionnaire is a dangerous practice, for it invites armchair statisticians like myself to find flaws in the questions. Much thought and prayer went into the questionnaire, but that is not to say it is perfect, or couldn't have been improved. We did our best to ensure that no bias or "I-can-tell-what-you-want-me-to-say" constructions were evident. Also, in the interest of statistical accuracy, subgroups containing less than ten members were normally lumped together with a "neighboring" group.

We are very grateful to all those who took their time to complete the questionnaires and also to the churches for giving up some of their valuable time to help in this task. The questionnaire follows. Its appearance has been substantially altered (different fonts, sizes, spacings, etc.) to make it fit into this book. You may answer the questionnaire yourself, treating it as a work sheet, and compare your answers with the others who completed it.

A Family Questionnaire

This brief questionnaire is to be used in gathering and analyzing information regarding current trends in Christian family size philosophies. After your answers have been correlated with those from others in your church and from other churches, different trends in the area of family size and birth control will be analyzed. This confidential information will be used in a book we hope to have published. Thank you for your cooperation!

1. Male _____ Female _____

2. Your age _____
3. Single ___ Married ___ Divorced ___ Widowed ___
4. Denominational affiliation: _____
5. Highest level of education: In High School ___ Graduated from H.S.___ In college ___ Completed undergraduate degree ___ In grad school ___ Completed one or more graduate degrees ___
6. Come from a Christian home? Yes ___ No ___ One parent ___
7. How many children were in the family in which you grew up?___
8. Did your mother work outside the home while you were growing up? Yes ___ No ___
9. How many years have you been a Christian? ____

This section is to be answered by those who are SINGLE.

10. Do you hope to marry? Yes ___ No ___ If you answered "yes," how many children would you like to have? _____
11. Why did you choose this number? Use the space below for your answer.
12. If you marry, will you be likely to use some type of birth control? Yes ___ No ___

This section is to be answered by those who are MARRIED.

13. Is your spouse answering this questionnaire too? Yes ___ No ___

14. How many years have you been married? ____

15. How many children do you have? ____

16. How many children would you like to have, ide-
    ally? ____

17. Why did you choose this number? You may use
    the space below:

18. Does your spouse agree with your ideal number?
    Yes ___ No ___

19. Do you use birth control (or if currently pregnant,
    will you use birth control after your delivery)? Yes
    ___ No ___

20. For wives (or husbands if your wife is not answer-
    ing this questionnaire): Do you work outside the
    home? Yes ___ No ___

21. (Optional for you, but helpful for us!) What is your
    family's annual income? Under $20,000 ___;
    $20,000-30,000 ___; $30,000-40,000 ___; $40,000-
    50,000 ___; $50,000-60,000 ___ over $60,000___

This final section is for EVERYONE.

22. Concerning the subject of sterilization as a viable
    form of birth control, please check all that apply to
    your beliefs: Allowable for either spouse ___; For
    husband only ___; For wife only ___; Not allow-
    able for either ___; I am sterilized ___; My spouse
    is sterilized ___; I plan to be sterilized ___.

23. What do you feel should be the determinative fac-
    tor(s) in a couple's decision on how many children
    to have?

24. Which has more advantages, a small family or a large family (small meaning three children or less)? Small ___ Large ___

25. Finally, to what degree do you believe the Bible addresses the issue of family size? Please rate on a 1-10 scale with a "1" being not at all and a "10" being a great deal: ____

Thank you very much for your help in this questionnaire. If you have any additional comments on areas that were or were not addressed relative to family size, please feel free to note them below.

I feel like the person in charge of planning for the church picnic; I'm bound to forget to pack something I should have remembered. Several of the questions have been broken down into subgroupings, but the one statistic *you* are interested in is quite possibly missing, like "How many people who have perfect pitch and make $30,000 to $40,000 per year, who come from non-Christian backgrounds, and who drive cars with diesel engines use birth control?"

Each question of the survey is addressed in the following pages, and, if apropos, commentary is provided.

General Demographics of Respondents

Number of Questionnaires Completed

253

Sources of Respondents

Churches — 63 percent

Bible College — 37 percent

Respondents by Age

Average age = 33.8 years
Church average = 39.7 years
College average = 23.6 years

Respondents by Sex

Male = 47 percent
Female = 53 percent

Marital Status

Married = 57 percent
Single = 37 percent
Divorced = 4 percent
Widowed = 2 percent

Education

Finished High School = 23 percent
In or Finished College = 66 percent
In or Finished Grad School= 11 percent

Background — Come From a Christian Home?

Yes= 60 percent
No= 33 percent
One Parent= 7 percent

How Many Children Were in the Family in Which You Grew Up?

The average was 4.2 children per family. Today's family is 1.8.

Average Number of Children Growing Up in Christian or Non-Christian Families

Average in Christian families = 4.1
Average in non-Christian families = 4.4
Average in one-Christian parent families= 3.7

It was a little surprising that non-Christian families of the last two generations would have had more children than Christian families.

Did Your Mother Work Outside the Home While You Were Growing Up?

Yes = 32 percent
No = 68 percent

Working Mothers, by Christian vs. Non-Christian

Christian mothers who worked= 26 percent
Non-Christian mothers who worked= 37 percent

Number of Children, by Working vs. Non-Working

The previous generation's mothers who were home-workers had half a child more than their outside-working counterparts — 4.3 to 3.8. That's not much difference, but there is a big difference when we bring really large families into play. Only 2 percent of the families with outside-working moms had more than seven children, while 8 percent of all *oikourgos* families did.

How Many Mothers Have Had Children?

All of them! (Just wanted to see if you were paying attention.)

How Many Years Have You Been a Christian?

The average was 15.9 years. When coupled with average age yields a surprisingly late average age of conversion — 18–years–old.

Statistics from the Singles Section

Do You Hope To Marry (under 35 years old)?

Yes = 98 percent

How Many Children Would You Like to Have?

3.2

The average number of children the coming generation of Christians wants is significantly fewer than the number their Christian or non-Christian parents had. If these single Christians follow through with their plans (and according to Wattenberg, the actual number of children couples tend to have is consistently lower than their pre-marriage dreams), the Cronkite 2088 election returns won't be worth hearing.

We originally combined the singles into five-year age groups for analysis, but then discovered that over 90 percent of the singles were under 30 years old. Those in their twenties (included in this age group for all following age group comparisons are also a few 18– and 19–year–old college students) wanted 3.3 children. The average for those few in their thirties was 2.9.

Single women hope for four-tenths of a child more than their male counterparts, 3.4 to 3.0, so no huge differences there, either.

In choosing their ideal number of children, the average single respondent did not limit himself or herself to a single choice, but most picked at least two possibilities (the average number of choices per person was 1.6). Next is a graph showing the range and distribution of the singles' choices.

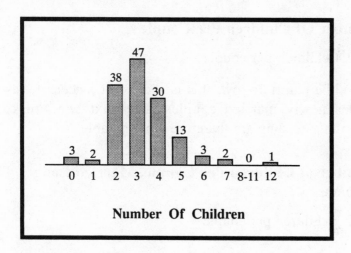

Number Of Children

Over four out of five choices were for two, three, or four children.

If You Marry, Do You Anticipate Using Birth Control?

Yes= 92 percent

No = 8 percent

One of the fascinating tidbits in this survey is this 8 percent group. When we checked each member of the group to see what their ideal number of children was, the average was a shocking 2.5 — much fewer than the 'yes' birth control group!

Statistics from the Married Section

Average Years Married

14.9 years

Number Of Children Per Couple

2.4 children per couple

While painfully low, this is somewhat inaccurate, as it includes newly married couples. The next two breakdowns under this heading are therefore more reliable.

Number of Children Per Couple, Married Longer Than Two Years

2.7 children per couple

Number of Children Per Couple, Over 39 Years Old

3.0

This statistic is more accurate than the two preceding it, as it gives a true picture of the average Christian family size in completed families. This represents a tangible drop from the previous generation's fertility and supplies the example for the

3.1 plans of the next Christian generation's fecundity (or lack of).

The Ideal Number of Children for Christian Couples

3.1

This is nearly identical to the desires of the single Christian. It also means that the great majority of married Christians (already with 3.0 children) have curtailed childbearing, *just one in ten planning to have another child.* Below are three subheadings dealing with this section; the ideal number relative to sex, to age, and the ideal relative to a couple's economic situation.

The Ideal Number of Children By Male vs. Female

Wives thought 3.1 children ideal
Husbands — 3.2

The Ideal Number of Children Figured by Age Group

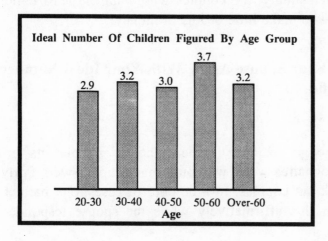

We find that the age of a couple has little to do with their perception of the size of an "ideal" family.

The Ideal Number of Children Figured by Family Income

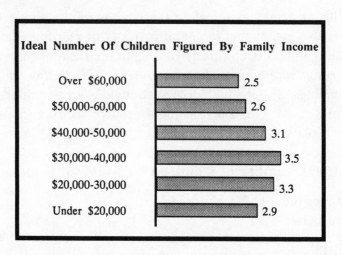

Ideal Number Of Children Figured By Family Income

Over $60,000	2.5
$50,000-60,000	2.6
$40,000-50,000	3.1
$30,000-40,000	3.5
$20,000-30,000	3.3
Under $20,000	2.9

Interestingly, the couples who want the least children are those who make little or lots of money.

Does Your Spouse Agree With Your Ideal Number of Children?

Yes = 85 percent

Though we had no idea who the people answering the questionnaires were, we could match up answers fairly easily to pick out couples. In a number of cases, one partner would answer this affirmatively while the spouse responded negatively!

Do You Use Birth Control?

Yes = 83 percent

This is the most poorly written question in the survey, as people who normally use birth control but are trying to have a child would answer no. *The Statistical Abstract of the United States (1987),* states that one woman in twenty-five is seeking to become pregnant. It may be that the percentage of Christians seeking to become pregnant is higher than the 4 percent in the *Abstract;* even so, the 83 percent seems low — by about 16 percent. In evaluating the questionnaires, we honestly found only *one* person whose answers gave any evidence of not having adopted a pro-birth control philosophy, and he was nearing retirement age.

Does the Wife Work Outside the Home in Your Family?

Yes = 44 percent

Following is the breakdown by age division.

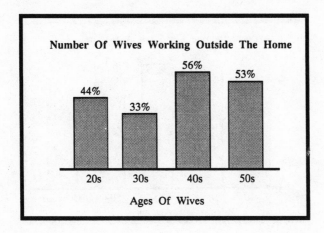

Married Money

The graphic below shows how the respondents divide on annual family income.

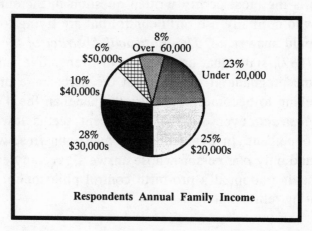

Respondents Annual Family Income

The average income for each age grouping is presented below. The figures were derived by averaging. For example, each couple making $20,000-30,000 was given a figure of $25,000.

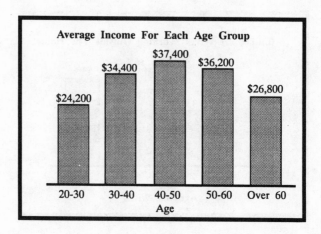

Average Annual Income for Two Paycheck Families vs. One

One paycheck families= $23,200
Two paycheck families= $33,900

Statistics from the Final Section of the Questionnaire

Sterilization

The respondents had several options in answering the sterilization question. They first had to decide who sterilization was permissible for; husband only, wife only, either, or neither. Here are the results:

Okay for either= 66 percent
Wrong for either= 31 percent
Okay for wife only= 3 percent
Okay for husband only= 0 percent

What follows is an attempt to understand the sterilization issue by examining it from four angles. Are women more likely to embrace sterilization than men; do certain age groups exhibit a propensity for it; is money a factor in the acceptance of sterilization; and could marital status play a part? The answers to these questions are displayed in four graphics:

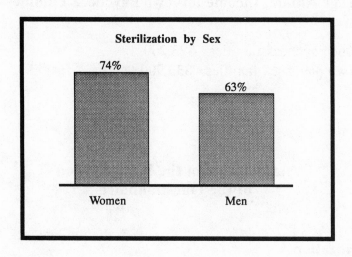

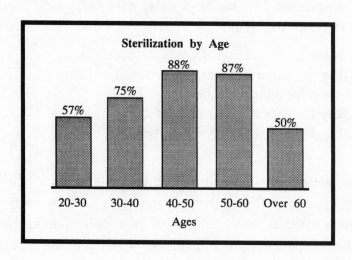

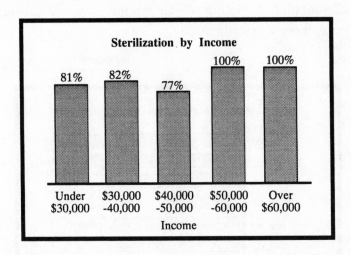

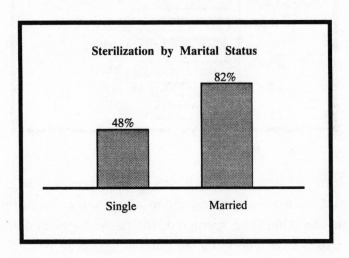

The next and final sterilization graph puts the preceding four all together, depicting which groups have the greatest or least acceptance of sterilization.

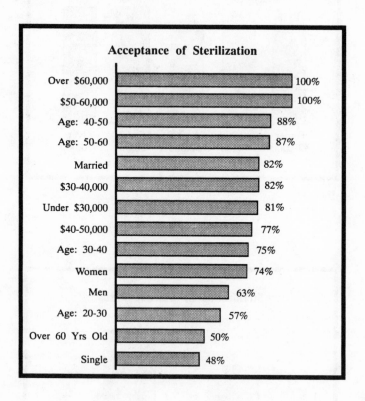

No matter how we slice it, sterilization seems to be widely accepted, with even our best group, the singles, almost evenly split on the issue. The average of the percentages in the above comparison is a whopping 76 percent, or three out of every four.

Now back to the end of the questionnaire.

Determinative Factors in Family Size Choices

After analyzing all the responses (16 percent of those surveyed gave none), there seems to be seven basic categories. They are listed below.

Financial = 54 percent
Personal reasons = 49 percent
God = 23 percent
Time = 15 percent
Health = 11 percent
Age = 4 percent
Career = 3 percent

A note of explanation relative to the above categories; "personal reasons" was basically everything that didn't fit anywhere else, but most of these were indicative of the idea that the decision whether a child was "To be, or not to be" was not really the question — couples were to decide on their own. The "God" listing included 'the Lord's leading,' 'the Bible,' 'God,' etc. "Health" covered physical and mental, the latter one being mentioned several times.

There were two other single responses to report. On the bright side, we found only one man who listed as a reason "overpopulation." On the darker side was the middle-aged youth worker who felt that all prospective parents should have to pass an exam and be licensed by the state.

Small vs. Large

This question was intentionally vague, inquiring simply, "Which has more advantages, a small family or a large family (small meaning three children or less)?" Due to lack of criteria, we hoped to get just a quick reaction to another question — "Which is *better,* small or large?"

We broke the sterilization question down into four groups. Here the small vs. large issue will be broken down into five, with four grouped together as was done in the final sterilization graph.

First, here is the total figure for all respondents:

Smaller is better— 62 percent
Larger is better— 38 percent

The fourteen subgroups represented in the next graph relate to Male/Female, Financial, Age, and Single/Married.

The following chart shows to what extent each of the subgroups believes that smaller families are more advantageous than larger families.

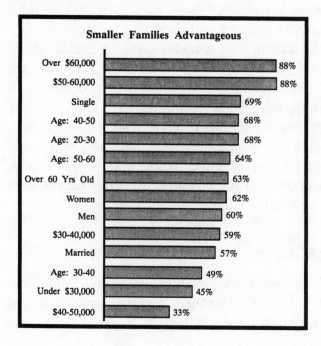

Some very interesting observations may be made when the two major charts (sterilization and small vs. large) are compared, group-to-group. One obvious thing, pointed out by a friend, is that most of the groups seem not to have thought out their positions very well.

The acceptance rate of sterilization was 76 percent. In the preference of small families over large the percentage is a lower 62 percent. Still, if this survey is at all representative of the church, as we believe is likely, three out of every five believers judges a small family superior to a large one.

We mentioned that small vs. large was broken down into five groups. The fifth compares those who grew up in large and small families (again, small meaning three children or less):

- 77 percent of those raised in small families favor small families.

- 51 percent of those raised in large families favor small families.

Among those growing up in families with six or more children, 62 percent said large families had more advantages. And those three fortunate singles who grew up in families with ten or more children were 100 percent sold on their life-style!

Rating the Bible's Family Size Content, 1-10

If the previous question was vague, this one was downright nebulous! No help or criteria was given, and several people failed miserably in their attempts to hide their disdain. After all the numbers were tallied, two things were obvious. First, different subgroups varied too little in their numbers to warrant charting, and second, the average was a nice average *4.5*.

Conclusion

Analysis of the data in this appendix yields very few surprises, unless perhaps the surprise is that there are no surprises; the statistical road is long and very smooth, with few
bumps — the young ladies under thirty do not want an average of six children, nor do couples making over $50,000 per
year. No group even wants four. Everyone is in the neighborhood of the high 2's to low 3's, and it is going to yield some
sparse neighborhoods. May God so move within the church
that the appendix for the next generation will look much
healthier!

DISCUSSION LEADER'S GUIDE

Anyone can lead a discussion group on *A Full Quiver*. Many additional questions and Biblical references for further study are given here. Also, questions for discussion and creative assignments are provided to help a leader.

If you are the leader, skim through this section and use the information in any order, or omit what you deem inappropriate for your setting.

A weekly outline follows:

Week One

Survey

A great way to introduce the concepts covered in this book is to have the class take the survey (see Appendix B) before they read the text. Confidentiality is important in a class setting, so no names! You may want to eliminate questions that could reveal the identity of a class member.

After the survey, discuss the questions (there will likely not be time to correlate them the same day they are taken, especially if the class is large). Are there any other questions that would be helpful to answer as a class?

The class leader will be in charge of correlating the survey results (or assigning the job to someone who enjoys statistics). If discussion is not too lengthy after the questionnaires are filled out, some statistical correlation can be done during the class by a class member.

Preparation for Chapter One

Read the four snapshots in chapter one aloud, and ask the class to respond to them. (Don't read the choices in the book.)

Week Two

Chapter One

Ask the class, "What things tend to make us react like Jake?" "What is your first reaction to imagining Jennifer's family?" Discuss why they have those feelings.

Preparation for Chapter Two

The results of one question in particular in the survey would be helpful to correlate before adjourning—Question #25: "To what extent does the Bible address the issue of family size (on a 1-10 scale)?" Try to get someone to tabulate these during the class period. Add up the totals and divide by the number of respondents to obtain the class average. Discuss your findings with the class.

Week Three

Chapter Two

In this foundational chapter we looked at a score of Biblical passages dealing directly with conception and who it is who conceives. But for space we left out over twenty-five other examples! Examine each of these and note any comments or insights you have.

Additional Scripture References

Genesis 17:20; 22:16–18; 26:4, 24; 28:3; 41:52; 48:4
Exodus 32:13
Leviticus 26:9
Deuteronomy 1:10–11; 6:3; 7:13; 13:17; 28:63; 30:5
Joshua 24:3
1 Chronicles 22:27
Psalm 105:24; 107:38; 26:15
Isaiah 44:2; 49:5; 51:2; 66:9
Jeremiah 30:19; 33:22
Ezekiel 36:10–11, 37; 37:26

Preparation for Chapter Three

List all the things God calls blessings in the Scriptures.

Week Four

Chapter Three

- How did God bless Obed-Edom in 1 Chronicles 26:4-5?

- Memorize Psalm 127:3–5 in your own translation. Then write a paraphrase of it.

- At the end of Chapter One study section, did you include children as one of God's blessings? How many of the blessings on your list does the world consider "blessings"?

- The *super* acid test to ask people is: How much would you have to be *paid* to have another child?

Preparation for Chapter Four

Current family size ideas in our culture differ from that of our history. Do you know of any of your friends who would not be around if their parents had only had 1.8 children?

Week Five

Chapter Four

Survey the church — if possible, ask your pastor or worship leader to do this from the pulpit. (It's great fun. Everyone will have a graphic illustration of the personal importance of allowing God to give more than three children!) Say, "Everybody please stand up. Would everyone who would not be here if your parents had had no more than three children please sit down. Now, would everyone who would not be here if your grandparents or great-grandparents had had no more than three children also sit down."

- How many or few of the congregation were left standing?

- This could also be done in a Sunday school class or large Bible study.

Preparation for Chapter Five

Could you trust God to control your family size?

Week Six

Chapter Five

- Why may a believer trust God to control his family size?
- Why might a believer not trust God to control his family size?
- What are some things that you have been afraid of trusting God with?
- What were the results when you did turn them over to Him?
- What is the relationship between obedience and feelings?

Preparation for Chapter Six

What questions or objections do you have at this point?

Week Seven

Chapter Six

Which of the following areas were of real concern to you before reading this chapter (circle all that apply)?

- Overpopulation and global depletion
- Christianity's adoption and acceptance of birth control
- Money
- "I can't handle more children."

- Social pressure

- Validity/necessity of careerism for Christian mothers

- Childbearing is a curable problem

- "Common sense"

- Acceptability of natural family planning

- Medical concerns

- Mother's age

- Cultural/Biblical arguments

- Adequate time for the kids

- Non-Biblical revelation

- God's sovereignty over Christian willfulness

- Societal reprobation

- Just a Roman Catholic teaching

- Fear (go ahead and join the club!)

- Safety of birth control methods

- Bible too quiet on the subject

Preparation for Chapter Seven

A young Christian husband or wife tells you, "I'm going to be sterilized next week so we won't have to have any more kids. What's wrong with that?" What would you say?

Week Eight

Chapter Seven

- How many couples do you know of child-bearing age who have undergone sterilization for the purpose of ending their ability to have children?

- If you know a sterilized couple, tactfully and lovingly ask them what the factors were leading up to their decision to be sterilized and if they have ever regretted their decision or contemplated a reversal (they may want to talk about it). Do not be judgmental — for "there but for the grace of God . . ."

- What should the church's role in sterilization be (before and after)?

Preparation for Chapter Eight

If you were (or are) single, what might you be thinking and feeling after reading this far in the book?

Week Nine

Chapter Eight

- How many young engaged couples follow this advice?

- What would your counsel be to a young man or woman who tells you their fiancee wants only 1.8 children while they would prefer God to give them 8.1?

- Evaluate the following statement: "The greatest stamp of blessing God could give to a new couple would be a child for their first anniversary present."

- What steps could a single man or woman take to change their attitude toward accepting children?

Preparation for Chapter Nine

What is your first impression of the father when you see a family with eight children in the grocery store? Why?

Week Ten

Chapter Nine

- This chapter mentioned that a man with a large family might be considered "out of touch with reality." Do you know any Christian families with six or more children? Have you heard yourself or others being critical of them?

- What lessons can we fathers learn from the Lord's example of how He poured His life into His twelve spiritual "children"?

- Consider some of the dads in the Bible (for example Noah, Abraham, Isaac, Jacob, David, Solomon). How did they fare as fathers? Rate them on a scale of one to ten (ten is the best).

- Now compare your ratings with others in your class (or with your spouse), and discuss why you rated them as you did.

- What advantages could there be if in six years you married men had three more children?

Preparation for Chapter Ten

Wives, without asking your husband, do you think he would like another child?

Week Eleven

Chapter Ten

- What concerns do women have regarding having more children?

- Central to the New Testament writings of Peter is the theme of suffering. What special sufferings do mothers have that fathers do not? How can God help with these?

- How does the importance of organization change as a family grows? How can women achieve greater organization in the running of their homes? (Read *All the Way Home* by Mary Pride for help with organization.)

- Consider Hebrews 10:24, 25. How do these verses relate to keeping sane with a large family?

- Is adult fellowship more important for the mother of seven children than for the mother of two? Why might it be?

Preparation for Chapter Eleven

What possible impact could this pro-family theology have on the future impact of the church?

Week Twelve

Chapter Eleven

- Why were Rachel and Leah so different from modern women in their desire for children? Which group seems the more Biblically-based?

- Is this a valid statement: Today the church does not love children. Discuss.

- Consider the Garden of Eden scene in Genesis 3:1–7. There are several enlightening analogies between the temptation in the passage and the temptation to demand reproductive control for ourselves. Think of the passage in terms of these issues.

ABOUT THE AUTHORS

R ick and Jan Hess are from Omaha, Nebraska, where they were high school sweethearts. After graduation Rick spent four years at Kansas University. While a freshman, he heard the Gospel and gave his life to Jesus Christ. He led Jan to Christ three months later.

They were married in 1972 and moved to Austin, Texas, where they lived for three years while Rick worked on his master's degree.

They returned to Omaha in 1975, and their eight children, Staci, Andromeda, Adam, Stefani, Daniel, Alexis, Micah, and Zachary have been born there.

They are presently living happily ever after.

The typeface for the text of this book is *Times Roman*. In 1930, typographer Stanley Morison joined the staff of *The Times* (London) to supervise design of a typeface for the reformatting of this renowned English daily. Morison had overseen type-library reforms at Cambridge University Press in 1925, but this new task would prove a formidable challenge despite a decade of experience in paleography, calligraphy, and typography. *Times New Roman* was credited as coming from Morison's original pencil renderings in the first years of the 1930s, but the typeface went through numerous changes under the scrutiny of a critical committee of dissatisfied *Times* staffers and editors. The resulting typeface, *Times Roman*, has been called the most used, most successful typeface of this century. The design is of enduring value to English and American printers and publishers, who choose the typeface for its readability and economy when run on today's high-speed presses.

Substantive Editing:
Michael Hyatt

Copy Editing:
Darryl F. Winburne

Cover Design:
Steve Diggs & Friends
Nashville, Tennessee

Page Composition:
Xerox Ventura Publisher
Printware 720 IQ Laser Printer

Printing and Binding:
Maple-Vail Book Manufacturing Group
York, Pennsylvania

Cover Printing:
Weber Graphics
Chicago, Illinois